Buy Gold Now

Buy Gold Now

How a Real Estate Bust, Our Bulging National Debt, and the Languishing Dollar Will Push Gold to Record Highs

Shayne McGuire

WILEY

John Wiley & Sons, Inc.

Published by John Wiley & Sons, Inc., Hoboken, New Jersey
Published simultaneously in Canada

Limit of Liability/Disclaimer of Warranty: While the publisher and author have used their best efforts in preparing this book, they make no representations or warranties with respect to the accuracy or completeness of the contents of this book and specifically disclaim any implied warranties of merchantability or fitness for a particular purpose. No warranty may be created or extended by sales representatives or written sales materials. The advice and strategies contained herein may not be suitable for your situation. You should consult with a professional where appropriate. Neither the publisher nor author shall be liable for any loss of profit or any other commercial damages, including but not limited to special, incidental, consequential, or other damages.

For general information on our other products and services or for technical support, please contact our Customer Care Department within the United States at (800) 762-2974, outside the United States at (317) 572-3993 or fax (317) 572-4002.

Designations used by companies to distinguish their products are often claimed by trademarks. In all instances where the author or publisher is aware of a claim, the product names appear in Initial Capital letters. Readers, however, should contact the appropriate companies for more complete information regarding trademarks and registration.

Wiley also publishes its books in a variety of electronic formats. Some content that appears in print may not be available in electronic books.

For more information about Wiley products, visit our web site at www.wiley.com.

Library of Congress Cataloging-in-Publication Data:

McGuire, Shayne, 1966–
    Buy gold now: how a real estate bust, our bulging national debt, and the languishing dollar will push gold to record highs / Shayne McGuire.
        p.   cm.
    Includes bibliographical references and index.
    ISBN 978-0-470-18588-9 (cloth)
        1. Gold.   2. Investments—United States.   3. Monetary policy—United States.
    4. Balance of payments—United States.   5. United States—Economic conditions—2001–
    I. Title.
    HG289.M375   2008
    332.63'28—dc22

                                                                        2007038102

Printed in the United States of America

10   9   8   7   6   5   4   3   2   1

For my wife, Winnie, and our children, Anna and Alan,
three wonderful people at the center of my life

Contents

Acknowledgments   ix

About the Author   xi

Introduction   1

Part One   Our Debt: American Financial Risk Has Never Been Higher

Chapter 1:   The $65 Trillion Wind Blowing from Our Future   11

Chapter 2:   How Can Families Really Be Getting Richer by Borrowing More?   15

Chapter 3:   Why the World Continues Lending (Most of Its Savings) to Us   23

Chapter 4:   Relying on Foreigners: Our Economic Future May Be Out of Our Hands   35

Part Two   Our Homes: The Epicenter of American Economic Risk

Chapter 5:   Real Estate, this Decade's Economic Driver, Could Drive Us into Recession   45

Chapter 6: The Negative Amortization Mortgage
Loan Is Born   53

Chapter 7: Tighter Lending Standards and the Fed
Can't Help   57

Chapter 8: The Great American Equity Cash-Out
Is Coming to an End   63

Chapter 9: Financial Culture Shock: Real Estate
Can Have a Negative Return   67

**Part Three   Our Economy: The Longest Economic
Boom Ever Is Probably Ending**

Chapter 10: Balance Sheet Recession: We Could Be Heading
in a Japanese Direction   75

Chapter 11: Smiling on the Lawnmower: Affluent Poverty   87

Chapter 12: As the Fed Cuts Rates This Time,
Could the Dollar Finally Collapse?   95

Part Four   The Case For Gold

Chapter 13: Why the Time Is Right for Gold to Skyrocket   109

Chapter 14: Stocks and Bonds Offer Little Compensation
for Risk Today   127

Chapter 15: Gold's Scarcity: New Sources of Demand
and Falling Supply   137

Part Five   How To Buy Gold

Chapter 16: When You Simply Want Financial Insurance   149

Chapter 17: Mining Stocks, ETFs, and GoldMoney   159

Chapter 18: Rare Coins: A Bet on the Highest
Possible Gains in Gold   169

Chapter 19: Why Silver Might Rise More Than Gold   187

Conclusion Don't Be A Gold Bug: Sell When It Is Time To Sell 191

Notes   199

Index   217

Acknowledgments

Many people helped me write this book, some without knowing it. First and foremost, I need to give special thanks to my loving wife, Alejandra (known to most as Winnie), whose constant encouragement and many efforts helped me complete it. My mother, Quinta Roberts, mostly through her endless love and care for our children, Anna and Alan, was indispensable. My father, Stryker McGuire, and his wife, Julith Jedamus, were of great help at vital points in the writing process, and Dad carefully read through the manuscript and provided editorial advice. I would also like to thank my brilliant and ever-dependable niece, Gabriela Alcalá, who took time away from her college studies to assist in formatting.

The book was helped tremendously by long conversations with my good friend Patrick Cosgrove, a stellar fund manager at Teacher Retirement System of Texas. And a great many Bloombergs and chats with my pal Marc Fleischman, a derivatives and fixed income specialist at Bear Stearns in London, were deep challenges to my convictions. At TRS, I am also grateful to Tom Cammack, who years ago first suggested I take a closer look at gold, and to Chi Chai, KJ VanAckeren, and Jim Hille, my mentor in fund management, who is no longer at the firm. Along with Patrick, the five stimulated many of the thoughts that went into the text through the many lengthy discussions about global finance we have had.

I would also like to thank Britt Harris, the Chief Investment Officer at TRS, for his interest and encouragement.

Much of what I know about precious metals investing and the arcane world of rare coins I owe to the experts at Austin Rare Coins. During the many hours I have spent there, Jay Bowerman, Ross Busler, Roxanne Byrd, Gabe Elton, Mike Gonzalez, Robert Kiser, and Mike Swingler provided hours of patient instruction about Saint Gaudens gold and Morgan Silver Dollars and the difference between business strike and proof, but I owe special thanks to Michael Byrd and Ryan Denby for permanently opening the firm's doors and friendship to me. Jeff Garrett, one of the premier authorities on rare coins, went out of his way to instuct me regarding several classic American rarities and George Cooper, a specialist at USA Gold, provided me with useful information on the history of gold confiscation.

I would also like to give my warm thanks to James Turk, one of the world's gold experts, for his observations and for revising my manuscript. Philip Newman, a senior metals analyst at GFMS, helped answer important questions about the global gold market and I would like to thank him for his help.

A great number of conversations, conference calls and emails with several brilliant economists and investment strategists over the years have been of great help in managing TRS investments and, indirectly, in writing this book. Richard Bernstein, David Malpass, Stephen Roach, and most recently Donald Luskin in the United States, Albert Edwards and David Owen in Europe, and Gerard Minack and Christopher Wood in Asia were minds to which I am fortunate to have had access. But I would like to give special thanks to Gerard, who kindly revised the manuscript and offered important suggestions.

I owe special thanks to my old friend Joe Harmes and to a new friend, Jim Moore, without whom *Buy Gold Now* might have remained on the drawing board. It finally left it with the help of David Pugh, my editor at John Wiley & Sons, whom I thank along with Stacey Small, Kelly O'Connor, and Michael Lisk for their patience and kind assistance in bringing my book to life. I am also grateful to Tim Moore, who carefully read through the text and provided useful insights.

Finally, I would like to thank Wanda Penn, the thoughtful landlord and now friend, who went out of her way to accommodate my sea of books and papers on the big table in the small room above her garage in Hyde Park where I wrote this book.

About the Author

S hayne McGuire is the Director of Global Research at Teacher Retirement System of Texas, one of the nation's largest pension funds with $115 billion in assets. With 15 years of international financial experience, McGuire has managed a $2 billion European equity portfolio and was ranked among the best Latin American analysts by *Institutional Investor* in 1995 and 1996. An avid gold investor, in recent years he has worked closely with Austin Rare Coins, one of the country's leading precious metals companies. McGuire graduated from Fordham University and holds a Masters in History and an MBA from the University of Texas at Austin. He lives in Austin, Texas with his family.

Introduction

Gold rose 2,300 percent over the nine years that ended in 1980, one of the most spectacular runs that any major financial asset class has ever recorded. If the 1990s Nasdaq rocket had surged as gold did, it would not have stopped at its peak of 5,049 on March 24, 2000. It would have doubled again to over 11,000. While gold initially rose because the U.S. government was unable to maintain its price fixed at $35 an ounce in 1971, it continued climbing so sharply and so fast because the gold market is tiny in the immense global financial ocean: a relatively small amount of investor interest was able to make it surge as stocks and bonds languished. Today, following the long years since 1980 during which gold has generally lagged other investments, the effect would be far more dramatic because the $140-trillion global asset market is so much larger. All the gold in the world is worth $3.4 trillion, yet only a small fraction of that amount is traded on financial markets. If one percent of the global value of stocks and bonds—roughly $960 billion—went into gold the precious metal would skyrocket. This amount is 18 times what the mining industry produces and substantially more than what is traded on gold markets during an entire year. There simply wouldn't be enough gold available at the current price. With gold still trading below the peak of $850 it reached almost three decades ago, thinking of prices well above $10,000 per ounce would suddenly become rational.

Athough it has been regarded mostly as a commodity over the last three decades, for thousands of years gold was the world's purest form of money and, being nobody's liability, the indisputable store and measure of value. Like U.S. Treasury bonds or cash today, gold was also seen as the ultimate escape from all financial risks, including the risk inherent in holding paper currency itself. But since 1971—that is, during less than one percent of the span of human civilization—all monetary value has ultimately been measured in U.S. dollars, the quantity of which are no longer limited by physical gold as had been required under The Bretton Woods monetary system that effectively collapsed in that year. Being the premier currency in virtually all of the world's central bank vaults, the U.S. dollar is the de facto foundation of the global monetary system, the metric used to weigh all other currencies, and hence the final measure of the value of everything that has a price. The dollar is the world's money.

But the world's money is not well. Another country's leader said many years ago that the dollar being the world's currency was an "exorbitant privilege" since it forced other nations to absorb American liabilities and fund our deficits.[1] But in the 1960s, Charles de Gaulle was speaking far too soon, as Vietnam War-induced deficits were negligible by present standards. The United States held a massive net international asset position and almost half the entire world's monetary reserves. Today, forty-three years later, the country's financial condition is entirely different. Our nation *absorbs* more than half of the world's savings to fund our current account deficit—since we now consume six percent more as a nation than we produce—and to do so, American debt to the world is growing like never before. Our once colossal net international assets have become a net liability of $2.5 trillion. International foreign currency reserves, which the U.S. Treasury Department reports weekly, are now lower than Mexico's.[2]

Figure I.1 shows that U.S. debt has grown to more than 300 percent of gross domestic product, a level last approached when thousands of banks were collapsing in the 1930s, which makes this picture all the more striking. Our GDP is not falling today as it was in the thirties—it

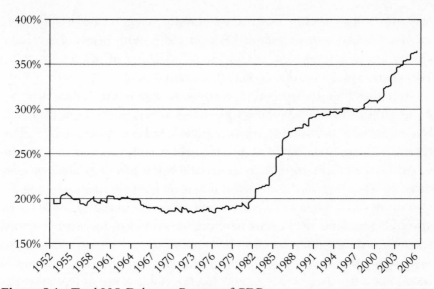

Figure I.1 Total U.S. Debt as a Percent of GDP
SOURCE: Total debt from Flow of Funds Accounts of the United States, Federal Reserve; GDP from the Bureau of Economic Analysis.

is our liabilities that are rising faster. Five dollars in debt are being added for each dollar in American GDP.[3] And while government liabilities are surging, what is happening to American consumers, who cannot raise taxes or lay off their spouses, is far more troubling: Household debt has more than doubled so far in this decade while inflation-adjusted wages have been stagnant for years. Debt payments each year are taking a larger share of American paychecks, which are already being battered by sky-rocketing healthcare costs.

For each of the last five years in which consumer debt has risen by an average of one trillion dollars, concerns have been brushed aside by a cheerful Federal Reserve revelation: The value of assets, primarily our real estate, has been rising faster than that of our debts. But to think that credit—not income growth—has made us wealthier than ever is becoming harder to believe now that the recent surge in foreclosures and homes for sale is causing the median American home price to fall for the first time since the Great Depression when we are not in a recession. And homes are where the bulk of American household wealth resides. Now that we are no longer winning the race with debt, perhaps it is time to take a long, hard look at the American balance sheet instead of expecting the next Fed rate cut to reignite the economy—with even more credit.

Is the U.S. economy so stretched by debt that we are on the verge of a balance sheet recession, one in which no amount of monetary or fiscal stimuli are sufficient to make consumers continue borrowing, such as occurred in Japan during the 1990s, or perhaps here in the 1930s? Will foreign central banks, bloated as they are with dollar currency and American liabilities, continue funding our deficits? Central banks have been forced to absorb trillions of deficit-driven dollars in new reserves this decade, each year injecting more liquidity into their own economies in an effort to maintain competitive currencies. Doing so has been vital: exporters to the U.S. need their governments to maintain what has become a vendor financing system—amassing dollars and lending Americans more money so that we can continue buying attractively-priced foreign products. But with Chinese liquidity becoming less manageable as a direct result and inflationary pressures rising, will our biggest lender finally be forced to stop buying our dollars?

This book examines these vital questions, which are intimately linked with present troubles in financial markets. The small problem in the U.S. subprime mortgage arena that has grown into an outright multi-trillion-dollar credit crisis had its roots in the increasingly unhealthy American balance sheet: Many consumers simply can't afford to make the higher payments on their reset subprime mortgages. And now it has become clear that a great many other Americans, some with jumbo mortgages, are also beginning to face difficulties. But serious problems began emerging further up the mortgage chain in 2007. The stocks of Fannie Mae and Freddie Mac, the heart and soul of the $22-trillion American real estate industry, lost more than half their value in just two months. Dozens of mortgage lenders have collapsed, and shares of Countrywide Financial, the country's largest mortgage lender, plummeted on fears that it could go into bankruptcy for lack of liquidity. But liquidity might be the least of our problems if the U.S. economy cannot withstand increasing levels of debt at *any* rate.

As Figure I.1 implies, since the 1980s the immense asset edifice of the United States was erected with significant reliance on credit, and credit has helped support the many productive efforts that have made us wealthier. But the currency with which our building was constructed is only as strong as our balance sheet, and growing doubts about our financial foundation could in time provoke an unparalleled catastrophe.

Approximately 60 percent of paper dollars circulate outside the United States and the majority of U.S. Treasury bonds are owned by foreigners.[4] Today we rely on the world's confidence more than ever. If faith in the dollar were lost, there would be no one to finance the $650-billion current account deficit in our saving-deficient economy. As a consequence, interest rates and inflation would likely soar, financial markets would fall very sharply as investors fled U.S. assets, unemployment would rise, and the economy would almost certainly go into a severe recession. The Fed could be powerless since cutting rates deeply would apply further downward pressure on the dollar, already at a record low; and raising rates might strengthen our currency but also ensure a recession in our debt-laden economy, which in time could also weaken the dollar.

The U.S. consumer accounts for a fifth of global GDP. Despite the rise of China and emerging markets as core players in the global economy, the world's reliance on U.S. consumer spending is stronger than ever. It accounted for 19 percent of world economic activity in 2006 compared with 17 percent in 1990 and 15 percent a decade before then. If the dollar were to collapse other major economies, which derive a substantial part of their growth from exports to the U.S., would suffer deeply as well. With the bond markets in disarray, there would be few places for the ocean of liquidity present in global markets today to hide, and prices of the few assets in which to take cover, like gold and other precious metals, would rise substantially. Although demand for gold should rise gradually in normal times, it would spike dramatically in a major currency crisis.

This book makes a case for buying gold as protection against the rising risks of an unprecedented global currency crisis provoked by the dollar. It examines our debt predicament, the U.S. real estate market, and the future of our economy, discussing some of the alarming issues that many economists are pointing to with concern. Gold rises when the risks inherent in holding paper currency increase, as they are doing today, and when stock, bond, and other investment returns are insufficient to compensate for climbing risks in financial markets. Bond yields remain near historical lows with the 10-year treasury bond offering barely 4 percent. Corporate profit margins are at 50-year highs (implying the stock market will struggle to continue climbing), the economy is slowing and with a great many other financial concerns rising, it is no wonder that gold broke through $500, and then $600 and $700 an ounce in the past two years.

But there are other reasons why the price of gold should remain strong. For one, supply has weakened. Gold mining production peaked in 2001, and the average global cost of producing a refined ounce of the ever-harder-to-find precious metal has doubled in just seven years. Central banks, which have dumped gold on global markets for decades—clearly to preserve the mirage of global monetary stability and faith in the dollar— have sharply reduced their precious metal sales in the last two years. Government gold sales fell 38 percent in 2006, and despite a rebound in 2007 Germany, the world's second-largest holder, surprised the market during the summer by announcing that it would not sell any more gold in that year, and it was followed by Spain a few months later.[5] Perhaps this decades-old policy of dumping gold on the market could be grind-ing to a halt out of concern for the sinking value of the dollar, or because they have been selling the precious metal for decades: There simply might not be much left that central banks want to cash in.

Would the monetary authorities of any country want to hold 100 percent of their reserves in paper currency? Probably not. Every single currency in human history, bar none, has fallen against gold. Perhaps the gold likely to be sold by the International Monetary Fund, in need of funding, may end up being bought by other central banks. Russia is a buyer, and not a small one anymore, and China and Japan, which possess by far the largest foreign reserve cache in the world—more than two trillion dollars—hold less than two percent of them in gold.[6] The world will notice if these economic powers turn their attention to gold and diversify their assets away from the dollar, as the investment world is doing today.

While supply has weakened, new avenues of demand have arisen, thanks mostly to gold exchange-traded funds, which allow more and more investors around the globe to buy and hold representative amounts of gold with the click of a mouse. Gold ETFs only began trading in 2004, and they are now present on several markets throughout Europe and Asia and will soon be bought and sold on most major exchanges. The growing affluence of India, the world's largest market for gold, has increased demand. And in 2007, Chinese citizens, proportionally the world's biggest savers, were allowed to trade gold legally for the first time.

Gold is a political and economic asset and a spike in its price would immediately raise concerns for every central banker. As a signal of intense risk aversion, a sudden, sharp rise in gold investment, which would likely accompany a decline in stock and other asset values, could lead to direct intervention to stop its climb. The U.S. government unexpectedly confiscated gold in 1933 as worried citizens—and foreigners—were attempting to flee the dollar, as well as most other paper currencies, during the Great Depression. Keeping this and other issues in mind, the final chapters of this book discuss the advantages and disadvantages of the various ways of owning gold, and securing wealth for the future.

Despite the pessimism implied in buying gold, the book in your hands proposes a unique investment opportunity arising in precarious economic times. There is a notable difference between being a pessimist and feeling pessimistic about present financial conditions. In retrospect, few would call Warren Buffett a pessimist for selling his stock portfolio—virtually all of it—in 1969. He was merely being pessimistic about the market's temporary overvaluation. The sage of Omaha liquidated Buffett Partnership and returned money to investors after a 1,100 percent return over the previous 10 years—five times better than the Dow Jones Industrial Average had returned. In 1970, the market promptly lost roughly half its value.[7]

But in the 1960s, Buffett escaped the financial markets to the shelter of dollars. Today, the dollar has become something altogether different and now there is increasing safety in gold.

Part One

OUR DEBT: AMERICAN FINANCIAL RISK HAS NEVER BEEN HIGHER

Chapter 1

The $65 Trillion
Wind Blowing
from Our Future

Perhaps the most alarming financial document written in American history was put on the Web for the public to see on December 14, 2005. Addressed to the president and members of the House of Representatives and Senate, the brief letter written by the comptroller general of the United States informed our leaders that every full-time worker in the country owes $375,000. This amount, which represents each worker's share of total federal government obligations, was 127 percent higher than what was owed just five years earlier, the letter explained.[1] However, it did not account for the gargantuan continuing expenses derived from Hurricane Katrina or the ongoing conflicts in Afghanistan and Iraq—wars whose ultimate costs some academics have estimated could run into the trillions.[2]

It was during this time—the federal-liabilities-doubling-in-five-years time—that the Bush administration began reporting a lower deficit (the government's yearly revenues less expenditures, not accumulating debt on the books) thanks mainly to soaring tax revenues derived from a strong economy. Ironically, it was also in these deficit declining/debt soaring times that then Treasury Secretary John Snow was forced to borrow from the federal employees' retirement fund for a few weeks as he waited for Congress to raise the government's statutory debt limit, which it dutifully did.[3] It was the fourth time the debt cap had been raised since President Bush had taken office.[4]

Is the deficit actually falling as federal debt gallops forward at the fastest pace ever (\$1.5 billion per day)?* It depends on how you do the numbers. The federal debt is \$9 trillion, or about six times that amount if you include the present value of all future promises our government has made (as Walker, the government's chief accountant, did for the calculation above). The White House reported a \$296 billion deficit for its 2006 fiscal year, or 2.2 percent of our GDP. But using generally accepted accounting principles (the ones required of American corporations to prevent them from deceiving the public) would make the deficit almost 10 times larger—\$2.4 *trillion*, or 18 percent of GDP.[5]

Even if we accept that the deficit is improving as our total national debt continues to climb, most economists believe the deficit is only taking a breather before the marathon, or as Federal Reserve Chairman Ben Bernanke suggested, it might be the "calm before the storm."[6] Beginning on January 1, 2008, an explosion of government spending was ignited by 78 million Americans. These are the men and women of the baby boom generation, born between 1946 and 1964, who are becoming pensioners and the medical beneficiaries of the proportionately declining younger generations that remain working.[7] It is to them, our future retirees, that America owes the most, a perhaps unpayable amount.

While the federal debt has just passed the mammoth \$9 trillion mark, this is peanuts compared with what is owed, the payments that will need to be made to the Social Security, Medicare, and Medicaid recipients in the years that lie ahead. Though estimates vary, the total national debt,

---

*See for yourself by Googling "U.S. national debt clock."

including these obligations, has been calculated to be as large as $80 trillion dollars.[8] A recent, more conservative estimate is that total government liabilities, funded and unfunded, are now $65 trillion. To put this amount into perspective, it is larger than the entire capital stock of the United States, all the land, buildings, roads, homes, automobiles, factories, bank accounts, stock certificates, and consumer durables that we possess.[9] Lawrence Kotlikoff, an economist at Boston University and researcher for the National Bureau of Economic Research, believes our debt is so large that in a study prepared for the St. Louis Federal Reserve, he openly asked the stunning question, "Is the United States bankrupt?"[10]

As government disbursements begin to skyrocket in the years to come, our leaders will in time be forced to reduce the benefits of America's old and/or raise taxes, an inevitability that even Bernanke has warned of.[11] How high would taxes have to rise? In 2002, a team of top economists, statisticians, actuaries, and fiscal analysts from the Treasury Department, the Office of Management and Budget, and the Federal Reserve estimated that taxes would have to rise a steep 69 percent to achieve "generational balance"—that is, to balance the government's future expenditures with its tax receipts.[12] By the way, this inconvenient fact was omitted from the president's 2004 budget for fear it would undermine a third proposed tax cut.[13]

Since entitlement programs like Social Security involve transferring wealth from the young to the old, it remains to be seen how willing future generations will be to pay for extravagant promises made in the past. Will the young accept an increasing tax burden when they realize that earlier generations paid proportionately much less in payroll taxes during their lives? You should expect to hear the term "generational fairness" bouncing around the media increasingly in the years to come, as some economists have pointed out.[14]

Some believe this "entitlement panic" has been blown out of proportion and that the United States is far from bankruptcy. Why? Because the government can simply break its promises to the tens of millions of Americans on the verge of retirement. Entitlement benefits like Social Security "are not a contractual government obligation in the sense that a T-bond is" and there is "no such legal right to Social Security", a *Wall Street Journal* editorial pointed out in response to the dire warnings of Kotlikoff, Comptroller General David Walker, and other economists.[15]

The dark implication is that government bond holders (like foreign investors, who today own more than half of the Treasury securities in circulation) have no need to worry. But American citizens face the possibility of being cheated by our leaders in what would become perhaps the biggest financial scam in world history: men and women of the most powerful nation that ever existed being denied promised tens of trillions of dollars. Such an outcome is unlikely, if anything because it would mean mass political suicide in Washington. There is no political wrath like that of an angry senior voter. But this just brings us back to the paying the bill problem, which will necessarily be resolved through sharply higher taxes, reduced benefits, or both.

The intensifying debate over entitlements, which should be alarming to the great many Americans who will rely on federal pension and medical support to live out their final years, makes clear that the time for tough decisions is at hand. In strong words for a man of his position, in 2007 Fed Chief Bernanke warned of a "fiscal crisis" unless the entitlement problem is addressed very soon, though it should have been dealt with "ten years ago."[16] A buoyant economy has allowed Congress and the president to continue increasing the federal debt, and very few of our leaders show concern that the $220 billion we are paying each year in interest alone is larger than expenditures on Medicaid or the combined total for all federal income-support programs.[17] However, in the next few years, as the baby boomer tsunami gains strength, the government will finally need to ask the public for deep financial sacrifices. But we have problems of our own.

Chapter 2

How Can Families Really Be Getting Richer by Borrowing More?

F or the first time ever, household debt is almost equal in size to all that we produce each year, our entire gross domestic product of 13.5 trillion dollars. Although American household liabilities have been climbing faster than GDP for many years now (especially during the go-go '90s), there was a sudden, sharper credit spike this decade. Total mortgage, auto, and other consumer debt doubled in the last seven years to reach 13.0 trillion dollars.[1] The brief recession of 2001, worrisome at the time with the stock market crash fresh in our memories, is seen now as one of the least painful in U.S. history, and the reason is clear: Though corporate investment fell deeply, our consumption, the economy's largest component, never slowed down. It grew steadily, driven almost entirely by debt.

To say "almost entirely" is not hyperbole. Non-managerial wages—that is, what roughly 80 percent of Americans earn—have risen less than five percent after inflation during this century, and incomes (wages plus benefits and other items) have risen only slightly faster. In fact, wages as a percent of corporate income are at their lowest in almost 50 years.[2] The concern that American family earnings are barely keeping pace with inflation has given rise to a host of sanguine Wall Street interpretations, like the idea that we live in a "Plutonomy"[3] in which the wealthy have become the primary economic drivers of prosperity, the implication being that we need not worry excessively about the financial health of the nation's vast majority that earn sub-six-figure salaries. (Though a subject for a different book, 2005 tax data showed the greatest U.S. income inequality since the Great Depression.[4]) Buy Louis Vuitton, whose stock has nearly doubled in dollar terms in the last four years, not Walmart, still at stuck around $50 a share. But even with the continuing acceleration in compensation for corporate executives, Wall Streeters and other highly successful individuals, overall American incomes continue to grow at a snail's pace in relation to our debt, as Figure 2.1 shows.

If you think that the United States must be getting poorer because we are borrowing much faster than our paychecks are rising, you are wrong, according to many experts. Citing Federal Reserve figures, economists frequently point out that despite rapidly climbing debts, we are in fact wealthier than ever since our assets (primarily real estate and financial investments) have been rising faster than our liabilities.[5] Hence, it would seem that a great many Americans have been acting rationally, encouraged by our financial advisors into "debt consolidation" (sucking money out of our homes to supplement our sluggish incomes) and credit-enhanced investment strategies (margin debt on the stock market is back at the 2000 peak).[6] If home values and the stock market are rising faster than our debt (and anyone with a pulse can borrow money), doesn't it make sense to increase borrowing to buy *more* real estate and exposure to booming financial markets? Why save when you can *invest* in more square footage, a second home, and Google and Apple shares?

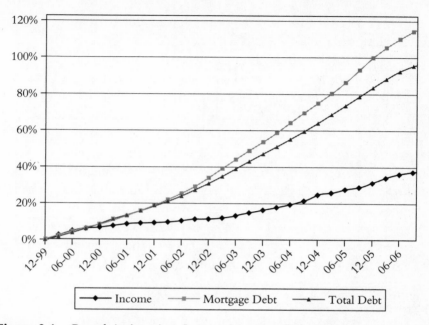

Figure 2.1   Growth in American Income, Mortgage Debt and
Total Debt Since 2000
SOURCES: Federal Reserve, Department of Commerce.

Looking at Figure 2.2, which shows that the American saving rate is close to zero for the first time since the Great Depression, you might think American finances are deeply concerning. You might be worried further knowing that the median family retirement account balance fell from $55,000 in 2001 to $27,000 in 2004, according to the Congressional Research Service.[7] But some experts would again disagree. Respected Bear Stearns economist David Malpass believes that the old-fashioned personal savings metric "doesn't really measure savings in the real sense."[8] He, like other economists, believes savings should include the realized gains from stocks, houses, and mortgage refinancing that offer a more realistic reflection of American family wealth, which has never been larger. Others add that savings metrics do not account for such immeasurable things as education and innovation. In national accounting, these are considered consumption, and not investment in what are the main engines of wealth-producing growth.[9]

Perhaps the saving rate needs to be adjusted, but even if it were inflated to include other items, this would not change the fact that

Figure 2.2   Personal Savings as a Percentage of Disposable Income
SOURCE: Bureau of Economic Analysis.

Americans have been putting less and less of their wages into the bank. Far more has been going into real estate, a more risky proposition than we once believed. Since much of the wealth Americans have accumulated in recent years is related to property, one needs to wonder what could happen if the real estate market crunch continues, a question so important that Part Two of the book is dedicated to the issue. We have invested in houses like never before, saving proportionately less of our earnings each year. And real estate is the most capital-consuming (mortgage, insurance, and maintenance expenses) and illiquid (hard to sell in a bad market) major asset a person can buy. Now that we have added $5 trillion in mortgage debt in just six years and locked it into hard-to-sell assets, have we become sitting ducks?

Though some Wall Street economists are beginning to show concern about household debt and falling savings now that signs of trouble are on the horizon, many generally remain optimistic (as I write in the summer of 2007), and recent history is on their side. The economy has thrived despite the many challenges faced over the last generation. Recessions have been relatively mild, employment is high, and despite apocalyptic predictions, the Savings and Loan crisis of the 1980s, the stock market crashes of 1987 and 2000, and even the 9/11 tragedy have not derailed the economy. Why should debt? In a book published in 1988—two long decades ago—Harvard Professor Benjamin Friedman warned of a credit excess-driven economic disaster, a concern praised at the time by three Nobel Prize winners, including Paul Samuelson, who commented that prosperity in the 1990s would "hinge on America's social thriftiness."[10] But thriftiness would have to wait, as well as the expected collapse. The Dow Jones Industrial Average—then near 2,000— is over 13,000 today, the economy more than double the size, consumer confidence far higher; unemployment is substantially lower, as is infla- tion. It's hard to bet against the optimists, and we have been winning the war with debt year after year.

Unfortunately, the bills are catching up with us. With sluggish wages and job growth now falling behind the number of new entrants into the workforce (as well as a weakening construction sector) only continuing high employment levels, tax cuts, and recourse to our credit cards and larger mortgages have been able to keep our consumption growing. However, our expanding debt has been showing signs of intensifying stress. Although we are not in a recession, late loan payments rose 10.7 percent in the second quarter of 2007, the biggest increase in 17 years.[11] And that report came months before the subprime crisis hitting the U.S. real estate market began in earnest.

Approximately 40 percent of all American corporate profits are derived from financial activities, a level double that of 20 years ago.[12] Since debt is now a bigger driver of the American economy, one has to wonder what would happen if credit began to contract, if Americans were forced to or decided to borrow less. Nothing, would say the roughly 50 million Americans who don't even have enough credit activity to get a credit score![13]

Unfortunately, a great many individuals and families carry larger debt balances than ever before, a fact that in time is likely to affect even the frugal. It is what economists call the "paradox of thrift": we need to continue spending to keep the economy humming along, and yet each of us also needs to limit consumption so that we can save for emergen- cies and retirement. Going beyond the zero-interest, zero-down strategy adopted by the auto industry in the wake of 9/11 to keep inventory moving, merchants like Rooms-To-Go, the national furniture chain whose ads feature a smiling Cindy Crawford, began offering customers a deal that only giving sofas away can beat: zero *payments* for years. How long can we go on borrowing from our future?

Perhaps the portion of our salaries that goes toward debt payments—which like total debt has never been higher at almost 20 percent—can continue to rise (see Figure 2.3). But even if we, as a nation, can withstand the pain of paying out even more to banks, will they be willing to continue lending on generous terms? As a result of foreclosures, particularly by those linked to subprime mortgages, the financial sector has begun tightening lending standards[14] and zero-down mortgages are becoming a part of the past. The subprime mortgage lending industry is on its knees, with more than 50 lenders already shut down or in bankruptcy[15], and the pain is moving up the chain into higher quality mortgages, like those offered to the wealthy.[16] After the deepest, longest, profit-making spree in banking history, financial regulators are beginning to show concern at the low levels of reserves at the nation's banks, which are needed to cover losses from loans that go bad. With reserves at a 17-year low, the Office of the Comptroller of the Currency, which regulates banks, recently let it be known that "there is risk building in the system."[17]

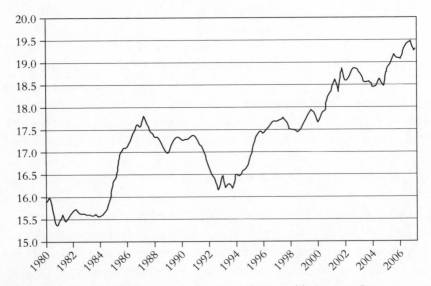

Figure 2.3 Debt Payments as a Percentage of Disposable Income Reserve
SOURCE: Federal Reserve.

The combination of exploding American household debt, sluggish income growth, and a negative saving rate has become a growing source of concern for many economists around the globe, which they refer to euphemistically as "imbalances."[18] Morgan Stanley economist Stephen Roach calculated that the U.S., though accounting for only 30 percent of the world's economy, added 98 percent of the cumulative growth in global GDP between 1995 and 2002.[19] Despite the growing importance of China and emerging economies in recent years, the U.S.—and the U.S. consumer in particular—remains the principal economic driver for the world. Our consumption—a whopping $9 trillion—accounts for 70 percent of our economy. This level is substantially higher than that of Japan (57 percent of its GDP), China (38 percent) or Europe (54 percent), all of which have ample savings and do not have trade deficits that need to be financed.[20] Lacking sufficient internal savings to lend to ourselves, we absorb much of the world's savings for our consumption. What would happen if the world stopped lending to us?

Chapter 3

Why the World Continues Lending (Most of Its Savings) to Us

Aggregating galloping government and consumer debt with booming corporate debt, one finds the world's largest economy with a balance sheet without parallel in our economic history. (See Figure 3.1.) The rising current account deficit (essentially a broader measure of the trade deficit) shows that our economy consumes 6 percent more than it produces each year, and this gap has been growing at an alarming pace over the last five years (see Figure 3.2). Our net foreign liabilities have climbed rapidly into the trillions in the last decade.[1] Speaking about our dilemma, Paul Volker—perhaps the most admired chairman in the Federal Reserve's history—said that he didn't "know of any country that has managed to consume and invest 6 percent more than it produces for long."[2] What is perhaps most striking and

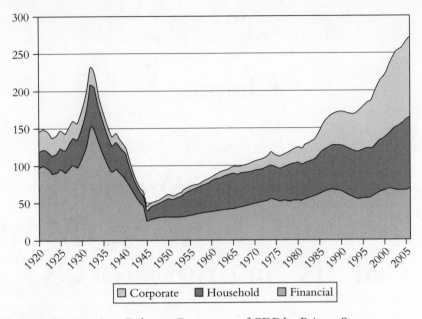

Figure 3.1   American Debt as a Percentage of GDP by Private Sector
Source: Morgan Stanley, Federal Reserve, Bureau of Economic Analysis.

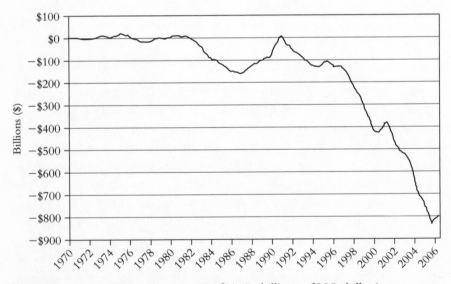

Figure 3.2   U.S. Current Account Deficit (in billions of U.S. dollars)
Source: Bureau of Economic Analysis.

unprecedented is that our current account deficit—funded by $2 billion in foreign capital each working day—absorbs most of the world's net savings.

If we were a smaller economy, our currency and financial markets almost certainly would have faced a crisis years ago as foreign investors fled our economy. So it was with Mexico in 1994, Thailand in 1997, Russia in 1998, and most recently in Argentina, where terrified depositors pulled $3.6 billion, the equivalent of 6 percent of GDP, out of their banking accounts in the last three days of November 2001.[3] In each case, the countries relied heavily on foreign investment (as we do today), and when they over-borrowed (thanks in large part to historically low interest rates, such as we have) concerned investors fled the countries' financial markets. The ensuing currency devaluations, despite assistance from the International Monetary Fund (IMF) and other countries, caused sharply higher interest rates and inflation, severe unemployment, and deep recessions.

Working in the 1990s in Mexico as an analyst at Barings (the British bank about to go bankrupt at the hands of a rogue derivatives trader), I remember the economic pain the country faced all too well: inflation went from 8 percent to over 50 percent, millions were laid off as many companies went out of business, and countless families lost their cars and homes as debt payments doubled due to skyrocketing interest rates. The corporate world was changed forever, and the entire banking system essentially folded and was ultimately bailed out by the government in a national emergency. Situr, a company I was about to begin covering at the time, went from being the largest tourism real estate developer in North America in December 1994 to having negative equity a few weeks later. Only a multi-billion-dollar bailout package led by the U.S. government, the largest we had ever made to a single nation, saved Mexico from the economic calamity that was imminent in early 1995.[4] A currency crash is the ultimate economic disaster.

Fortunately, the U.S. economy is so large and our financial system so resilient that far more than a few frightened investors would be needed to make the dollar tumble. Despite our deteriorating net international investment position (the fact that our foreign liabilities are larger than our foreign assets) American financial markets are large and deep, with nearly $50 trillion in total assets. Total household assets of $64 trillion are larger than global GDP; the real estate market alone is valued at an astounding $22 trillion. One-third of the world's stock market value is traded in the United States. Oil, and virtually all commodities like copper, wheat, and gold are traded in dollars. The U.S. Treasury 10-year bond yield is respected by decision-makers around the world as the ultimate *risk-free rate*, a foundation for the valuation of any financial asset, the benchmark to which the bonds of all the world's governments are compared. An economy-crushing currency crash has simply never happened since Federal Reserve notes began circulating as the national paper currency, even in the darkest hours of the early 1970s. Our centuries-old financial and political institutions have endured and strengthened despite all catastrophes, an achievement few nations can claim. And those believing the euro is rising to replace the dollar as the world's currency need to be reminded that the European currency is not even a decade old, and it has yet to face a major crisis.

That we have escaped the pain of a sudden and severe devaluation is, I believe, partly a reflection of still trusted economic foundations laid down decades ago, when the United States was the undisputed supreme economic power. Though we have become the world's largest debtor, the United States effectively remains the lender of last resort to all nations, a condition initially created when the United States emerged from World War I with its productive capacity virtually intact compared with the devastation facing other major economies. In the decade following peace at Versailles in 1919, it became the largest exporter, importer, and investor, and yet, as one historian put it, the "United States mattered a great deal more to the world than the world did to the United States."[5] Even when, to the great concern of the financial community, President Franklin D. Roosevelt actively tried to *make* the dollar fall and ignite inflation to push up collapsing cotton and wheat prices during the Great Depression, ultimately he was unsuccessful.[6]

In fact, the terrible price *de*flation that caused countless bankruptcies in the banking system and the agrarian United States were in large part a result of the dollar's *strength* vis-a-vis other currencies in the 1930s. Even during these troubled times, by 1933 the United States had amassed 43 percent of all gold held by central banks and by the end of World War II that percentage would grow to 60 percent. In fact, by 1948 the country held more than two-thirds of all the world's monetary reserves.[7]

In an era when gold was declining as the preeminent symbol of financial strength and solvency, the U.S. dollar was rising to take its place.

It was American economic dominance that permitted the creation of a new type of monetary system to replace the Gold Standard, which the powers-that-be were forced by economic circumstances to abandon completely in the 1930s. Under the Gold Standard, which governed financial transactions for three decades before World War I, currencies of the world's dominant economies were convertible into gold, a financial arrangement that facilitated global trade, kept interest rates low, and encouraged business development and economic expansion—as effectively all major currencies were as good as gold at a fixed rate. Only weaker economies went off gold, and each tried to do so only temporarily. Though not without its problems, the Gold Standard encouraged governments to maintain balanced budgets, since any signs of strain would prompt concerned investors to cash in a given currency for gold, thereby driving up interest rates and weakening the country's economy. And yet, at some point higher interest rates would attract investors back into a country's currency, as the government rebalanced its budget, so gold would return and be converted back into the higher-yielding currency, restoring balance.

But the system's stress test came with the advent of the Great War in 1914, which forced many governments off gold into deficit spending and created great financial uncertainty. As if anticipating its future might, the United States successfully defended the dollar's convertibility into gold at the war's outset, thanks mostly to a clever Treasury secretary who shut down the stock market, preventing Europeans from selling American securities in panic and converting proceeds into gold.[8] But the war caused investors to lose confidence in paper currencies and the rush into gold led virtually all nations to abandon convertibility— temporarily, the world had hoped. However, the return to the Gold Standard in the 1920s proved short-lived. The beginning Depression and need for deficit spending forced the world off the standard for good, and decades of monetary instability would follow.

To restore international financial balance following the collapse of the Gold Standard, the end of the Great Depression, and World War II, the new dollar-centric monetary system that had been put in force required that each country maintain its currency value within one percent of a set exchange rate with the dollar.[9] Thus, countries like Canada, France, and Japan regulated the value of their dollars, francs, and yen (which directly affected each country's interest rates, inflation, and economic growth) by buying and selling the U.S. dollars they each held in reserves, much as each had done with gold before. Hence, the countries most effective at maintaining currency stability tended to be those holding the largest reserves of U.S. dollars. Greater currency stability led to lower interest rates, which encouraged higher economic growth. The United States, meanwhile, was required to maintain a fixed exchange rate with gold so that any country concerned about the value of the dollar could simply exchange its U.S. currency for physical gold at a fixed rate of $35 an ounce. As long as our government maintained this exchange rate, countries ideally would be indifferent between holding dollars or gold as reserves. The dollar was to be as good as gold.

Though exchange rate volatility remained extreme and a round of competitive devaluations erupted in Europe during the late 1950s, the dollar-based Bretton Woods System (named after the place in New Hampshire where the international agreement was made) held together in the first years following 1945.[10] However, a fundamental problem absent during the Gold Standard years soon became apparent—while gold cannot be printed, dollars can. Having discovered the power of the printing press, American leaders began to realize that they could spend each year just a little more than the budget had projected. The roots of our present dilemma began growing as the United States created the world's money by expanding its liabilities to other countries, and our budget deficit began to rise. Between 1949 and 1959, $8.5 billion in reserves were created through a $7 billion increase in American liabilities.[11]

The vast monetary assets held by the United States after World War II were gradually being transferred to other nations, and our net asset position began declining. The world was now beginning to fund our borrowing and as the Vietnam War intensified in the 1960s, with the consequent surge in military expenditures, our budget deficit began to climb ever higher, funded by foreign central banks and investors. Though extremely low by today's standards, the growing deficit, which forced demand to rise faster than the economy's supply, began to cause inflation, inflation that we exported to other countries via the dollar.

Given the United States' weight in the international economy and the resulting synchronization of countries' business cycles, other central banks were forced to follow the Fed's lead.[12] But U.S. dominance combined with the government's continuing Vietnam War-driven expansionary policy began to cause concern among world financial leaders. France led the charge in criticizing the U.S. for requiring the world to fund its deficit spending, and in the 1960s the European nation began converting its dollar holdings into gold, effectively forcing the American government to begin selling down its massive holdings. Gold, the French Finance Minister at the time explained, is "the only monetary element outside the scope of government action,"[13] implying that the dollar was rapidly losing credibility as a store of value for political reasons that pertained to the United States, not the global monetary system.

Despite President Lyndon Johnson's assurances that he would defend the value of the dollar (that is, ensure that gold stayed at $35 an ounce by dumping the precious metal on global markets), a gold rush was gaining force. Though American citizens were prohibited from owning gold bullion at the time (they were limited to buying jewelry and rare coins, which were already climbing rapidly in value), foreign central banks and individuals began amassing large amounts. The fever was fed by a flurry of articles in the world media and by books on gold. Economists monitoring the amount of dollars in circulation reported a troublesome trend—more and more dollars in circulation and a declining amount of gold in U.S. vaults with which to back the American currency's value. By 1971, the flood of dollars into gold and other currencies, like the German mark, had become unsustainable. And in that year President Richard Nixon, facing the prospect of a complete depletion of gold from Federal vaults, ordered the closing of the "gold window": foreign central banks could no longer convert their U.S. currency into gold. The dollar was suddenly no longer as good as gold and the Bretton Woods international monetary system collapsed.

But it was not really a collapse, at least not one against world currencies. Pessimists expecting a dollar crash were right at first, as the dollar fell 30 percent against the deutsche mark during the first six months after the Nixon shock.[14] However, one thing had not changed at all: the world's dependence on the United States—and the American consumer in particular—the largest single source of economic demand the world has ever known. To continue selling Americans Japanese electronics, German cars, French wine, and Swiss watches, these products' prices needed to remain accessible to consumers that would purchase them in dollars. The dollar could not be allowed to fall.

Here's why. If Sony had been selling a television for $100 in the U.S. and making a 10 percent margin, the Japanese company would be devastated if the dollar fell 30 percent against the yen. Why? Because it would mean Sony's revenue in yen would fall by roughly the same amount wiping out its profit, and if it raised its prices by 30 percent to compensate for the lower dollar value and meet its yen-based costs, U.S. demand for the more expensive $130 TVs would plummet, and perhaps give American companies incentive to begin competing with them.★ Sony, like Mercedes Benz and French wine exporters, needed their governments to intervene in currency markets to support the value of the dollar, or put another way, to keep their own currencies weak. The world's exporters needed the dollar to be protected so that they could continue selling to the globe's largest market. U.S. consumption, even today, accounts for one-fifth of global GDP.

The world, then as now, relies on a strong dollar to keep the global economic engine running. This monetary truth was revealed bluntly in 1971 by then Treasury Secretary John Connally in a meeting with European envoys to Washington: "The dollar is our currency, but your problem." What he effectively meant was this: When the Federal Reserve, in an effort to increase economic growth, turned on its money-printing machine—and it was running at high speed in the 1970s—the Bank of Japan and Germany's Bundesbank had to do the same, or at least nearly the same.

More dollars in circulation caused U.S. inflation to reach 8.8 percent in 1973, more than double the previous year's rate, and it would soon climb to over 12 percent, a factor which formed a dark cloud of suspicion over the Fed. (Interest rates had been maintained extremely low in 1972, making it a great economic year—the year of Nixon's run for

---

★These amounts were presented for visual simplicity. But to be precise: if a value falls from 100 to 70, representing a 30 percent decline, the rise from 70 back to 100 requires a 43 percent increase. It's easier to fall than to rise.

reelection—and then Fed Chief Arthur Burns was a Republican like the incumbent president.[15]) The spike in inflation, a result of domestic (and probably politically-motivated) decision-making at the Fed, spread to the rest of the world. Foreign central banks had to absorb part of the U.S.'s monetary expansion, and they did so by accumulating even more reserves.

This continued even into the 1980s, when the dollar was very strong. Then Fed Chairman Paul Volker had caused the currency's value to soar with sharp interest rate increases aimed at taming accelerating inflation, until, as the Fed's vice chairman at the time said, "the darned economy just fell off the cliff" into the deepest recession since the Great Depression.[16] Although foreign money began flooding the U.S. bond market, attracted by high double-digit yields, the Reagan White House launched a tax-cutting campaign that, though successful in bringing the country out of recession, ultimately caused the federal budget deficit to surge like never before. This once again brought out dollar-crash predictors, but they were proven wrong (like their predecessors in the 1960s and 70s) as the 1980s dollar rocket took off. After rising almost 70 percent versus other currencies by April 1984, when experts began forecasting a decline, the dollar shot up, NASDAQ-like, another 25 percent over the subsequent 11 months.[17] President Reagan, warned by Democrats of potential damage to the dollar by his budget deficits, just sat back and chuckled, basking in reelection contentment. It was not until the September 1985 Plaza Accord of international ministers and central bank governors—and their coordinated market intervention to push the dollar down—that foreign exchange traders began a sustained large-scale reversal of their dollar trades.

But the strong dollar in the 1980s did not mean that the United States balance sheet was somehow improving. The budget deficit, as well as climbing consumer and corporate debt, finally pushed the country's net international investment position (the sum of what we own outside the U.S. less what we owe to foreigners) into the red for the first time in 1985. The personal saving rate, which had held above 8 percent during the troublesome '70s, was now falling—and it has not stopped falling since. Foreign central bank reserve accumulation paused in the 1980s, but as Figure 3.3 shows, countries like Japan continued accumulating American liabilities—that is, lending to us—at an increasing pace.

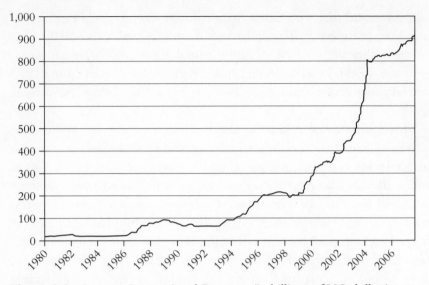

Figure 3.3 Japanese International Reserves (in billions of U.S. dollars)
SOURCE: Bank of Japan.

In a way, the world's continual accumulation of American liabilities would in time reveal itself as a trap for the nations most dependent on exports to the United States. Figure 3.3 shows the level of Japan's international reserves, the bulk of which are held in U.S. dollars. As the upward trend implies, Japan has not collected on the debts it has made to us—it has been increasing them—and the reason is evident: By cashing in dollars for yen, Japan would make the yen appreciate and cause pain for companies like Toyota and Canon, which bill their customers in dollars to be sent back home. But these accumulating dollar assets are not being spent on U.S. goods and services. Japan's obsession with maintaining a weak currency has created a "growing hoard of claims on the outside world" that are not being held in yen; they are "being accumulated in the fiat currency of the world's leading debtor nation, the U.S. dollar," explain Akio Mikuni and Taggart Murphy in *Japan's Policy Trap*.[18]

To keep the economy running as it does, Japan must maintain massive current account surpluses (in a sense, never fully enjoy its wealth) that allow—and what's more—encourage the United States to consume beyond its means and increase its debt to the world. And so far, a limit has not been found. Between 2003 and March of 2004, Japanese monetary authorities created 35 trillion yen out of thin air, or roughly $2,500 for every person in that country, and used it to buy a colossal $320 billion dollars, an amount sufficient to fund 77 percent of the U.S. budget deficit for fiscal 2004. "The Fed did not create money to finance a broad-based tax cut [in the U.S. that year]. The Bank of Japan did," explains economist Richard Duncan.[19] He jokingly asked if the Bank of Japan has actually become a branch of the Fed, the Federal Reserve Bank of Tokyo.

But, to continue the not-so-funny joke, the Fed has in effect been opening other branches, as China, Russia, Brazil, and a great many other economies have been amassing trillions of dollars in reserves. This has continued to maintain a relatively stable (yet declining) dollar, which encourages continued lending in the U.S. economy thanks to the low interest rates that our foreign friends have directly and indirectly facilitated. What would happen if they ever decided to cash in their dollars?

Chapter 4

Relying on Foreigners:
Our Economic Future
May Be Out
of Our Hands

L ooking down from the debt mountain we have been building
since the Bretton Woods Agreement was signed more than
60 years ago at the historical peak of American financial strength,
initial worries about central bank reserve accumulation of dollars the
Fed was printing seem almost childish. During the decade that ended in
1959, central bank reserves grew at a compound annual rate of 1.5 percent, an amount that was beginning to provoke some concern among
economists at the time.[1] But with a balanced budget, a healthy trade surplus, and a net foreign investment position that was larger than most

economies, a slight increase in American debt to the world was barely a concern. Economists at the time had no idea of what lay ahead.

Today, reserves are growing at more than ten times that rate, and the United States adds five new dollars in debt for every dollar in GDP.[2] We have a negative international investment position that is now larger than the GDP of China. Lacking sufficient savings to lend to ourselves, our source of funding is the rest of the world. Though at the end of World War II, we held two-thirds of all the world's international reserves, after decades of decline today we have less than a number of smaller economies.

The United States is the only major economy that has actually been *cashing in* reserves in recent years.[3] Meanwhile, countries like China, Singapore, Taiwan, Japan, India, Poland, Russia, Mexico, and Brazil, have more than doubled their reserves in this decade—and several have quadrupled them. Most of these reserves are being accumulated in dollars, which reflects the fact that our liabilities to the world have been growing more rapidly than ever. (See Figure 4.1 and Figure 4.2.)

An increase in reserves has long been seen as a sign of growing economic strength and a solid currency. But today it is less indicative of these

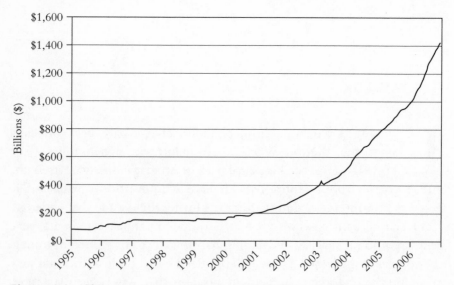

Figure 4.1   Chinese International Reserves (in billions of U.S. dollars)
SOURCE: The People's Bank of China.

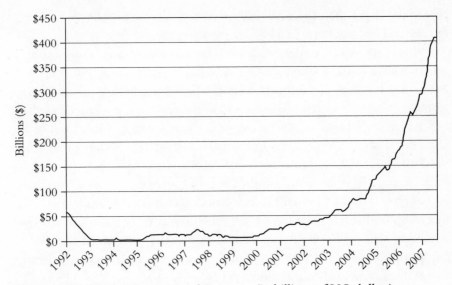

Figure 4.2   Russian International Reserves (in billions of U.S. dollars)
SOURCE: IMF.

nations' strength than a sign of the largest economy's weakness: The world's smaller but rapidly-growing nations have been forced to buy trillions of dollars from the mightiest not to defend their currencies from a devaluation, but to *defend the dollar from a collapse.* "There can be little doubt," said Bank of International Settlements General Manager Malcolm Knight in 2006, that "most of the recent accumulation of official international reserves has resulted from purchases of dollars to limit the appreciation of the currencies of a number of countries."[4] Had the world's major exporters to the United States—that is, every other leading economy—not been accumulating dollars, their yen, yuan, and rubles would have appreciated far more than they have already, making their export products less competitive.

As we have seen, the world's surplus nations—that is, the world's strongest economies, excluding the U.S.—have long been in a race to keep their currencies weak and the dollar strong. But I think the galloping dollar reserve accumulation, the funding of American deficits, and accumulation of dollar debt has gone from a healthy, international balance-of-payments arrangement into the truly bizarre. China added $136 billion in reserves in the first quarter of 2007. To get a sense of what this means, this amount is larger than the $140 billion in reserves that *all the central banks in the world* accumulated in 1987 *during the entire year.*[5]

"Nobody really understands the international monetary system," Johannes Wittenveen, the former managing director of the International Monetary Fund once famously remarked.[6] I think economists have yet to reach a verdict on the reserve phenomenon because something like this has never happened, and there is no precedent to look back at to compare it with. The trillions in reserves—effectively dollars printed by the Fed—that nations have accumulated in just a few years has yet to cause a surge in inflation (though it is now rising rapidly in China) and global growth has remained healthy. Much like it was difficult to predict that the 2000 stock market was a bubble about to burst, there are few observers willing to openly address the potential dangers of the global explosion in dollar reserves. Is this not simply excessive money printing that will in time lead to inflation?

The optimistic interpretation of the reserves phenomenon is that it is a new monetary paradigm, a Bretton Woods II, where deficit countries needing investment capital (the United States) attract funds from those that have large surpluses, like China. But let's face it: It's basically Asian vendor financing of U.S. *spending* capital. "The situation keeps their factories running, employs their people, allows cheap goods to come to America and America pays them with an IOU. They file that away in a dusty drawer somewhere and everybody is happy," explained Martin Barnes, a Canadian economist, a few years ago.[7] This happiness is perpetuated as China recycles its dollar reserves into U.S. debt instruments—it actually helps drive down our interest rates, facilitating our consumption and borrowing even more.[8] We don't need to save as much as we used to because we have Chinese savings, and the continuing strong world economy is proof that Bretton Woods II works, in this benign view of the world economy.

Less optimistically, I think of the global reserves balloon enigma as the Monopoly money phenomenon. In Monopoly, the popular board game, players use paper money printed in several colors to buy up a multitude of properties and pretend to be rich. But obviously, players could never use Monopoly money to buy real goods. Similarly, the trillions in U.S. liabilities (issued in terms of paper money unbacked by anything tangible, like gold) that the world's central banks are accumulating can never be redeemed for real goods without potentially causing a dollar collapse. And in that sense, China, the largest foreign creditor to the United States, effectively holds close to a trillion Monopoly dollars in its vault, money that effectively cannot be used in the real world.

But what if Chinese leaders change their minds and decided to begin cashing in their greenbacks? Buying hundreds of billions of dollars in recent years, China now holds about half its GDP in reserves—a whopping $1.2 trillion—a significant part of which are held in many types of American securities: U.S. Treasury bonds, American mortgage and corporate debt, and very possibly a slice of every other major form of debt we have—from credit cards to mobile home mortgages.[9] With every month that goes by, China owns more U.S. assets—billions more. If Chinese authorities decided to stop accumulating dollar assets—or, in a dramatic reversal—decided to actually collect on its American debts by dumping our bonds on the open market, this could cause interest rates to soar rapidly in the United States and perhaps cause a market panic and ultimately a recession. China is now, after all, the biggest single international buyer of dollar-denominated assets.

Politically, there are more and more reasons why China might decide in time to use its trillion-dollar reserve arsenal against the United States—that is, to stop lending us money and begin collecting. With Democrats now in control of Congress, the U.S. government has already begun applying trade sanctions against China claiming unfair competition with American industries, and a trade war is not out of the question. Both Fed Chairman Ben Bernanke and White House officials have been pressuring China to strengthen its currency at a faster pace, implying that the Asian nation is using the yuan to gain advantage for its exports at the expense of U.S. companies. Internally, the Chinese government is facing pressure from citizens that openly question China's trillion-dollar investment when there are many other uses to which the massive funds could be put. Finally, the sheer size of its dollar holdings might cause authorities to reconsider their portfolio allocation. At the present pace, China should hold $2 trillion in reserves—a stunning amount larger than its own GDP—within a year or two. Will they go to $3 trillion? Will other countries, which are also buying dollars at the fastest pace ever, also begin to reconsider their relationship with the world's largest debtor, whose balance sheet deterioration seems to be out of control?

I think financial markets, which are the ultimate judges of currency value, are already reaching a decision for them. As American travelers to Europe know all too well, the dollar's purchasing power has fallen substantially at Swiss watch shops, Harrods in London, and Parisian bistros. (See Figure 4.3.) Tooth decay versus paying seven dollars for dental floss was a value comparison I was forced to confront in France not long ago. Shopping has also become more expensive recently in unexpected places: The Indian rupee is climbing against the dollar, as is the Mexican Peso. In Brazil, where not too many years ago virtually worthless currency notes could be seen lying in gutters, the real is rising, a sign of financial disdain for our greenbacks. Foreign stock markets continue to outperform U.S. markets mostly because of the foreign exchange effect—their currencies strengthen as ours weakens.

Although the world needs a strong dollar, Americans have become completely dependent on foreign borrowing to sustain our lifestyles. Perhaps central banks, bloated as they are with dollars, can continue propping up the U.S. currency by dumping massive amounts of their own currencies onto the market, creating more of the abundant international liquidity that Wall

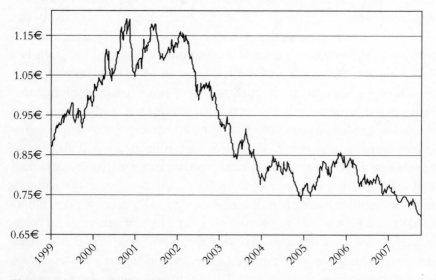

Figure 4.3 U.S. Dollar in Euros
Source: Bloomberg.

Street refers to lovingly, though none of us know precisely what the term means anymore. (What do American monetary measures M1, M2, or M3—the traditional measures of liquidity—reveal when so many of the dollars that exist today circulate outside the United States?) Two trillion dollars are traded daily on the foreign exchange market, and if investors collectively decide that the dollar is going to crash, it will be difficult for authorities to prevent it despite their success up to now.

If massive private dollar selling continues and central banks are forced to go from buying hundreds of billions of dollars a year to trillions—as the current pace of Monopoly money accumulation implies—the trend is likely to provoke a replay of the 1970s monetary disaster, in which all currencies crumbled as they chased the dollar down. And since there is no pure monetary metric to fall against, a collective currency devaluation means a surge in the price of gold, the only money that cannot be printed. To what other liquid store of monetary value could investors of over-printed paper currencies flee?

When all currencies collapse, physical assets soar as savers run away from paper money, protecting themselves from expected accelerating inflation. Since excessive money creation causes paper money to lose value, often at an accelerating rate, investors and the general public in time realize what is occurring and scramble to buy scarce assets, anything tangible whose value might be preserved as paper assets lose value. In the 1970s, this included illiquid assets like real estate, antiques, and art, as well as liquid ones like commodities and precious metals; all of these fared far better than the troubled bond and stock markets. But, although the reserves phenomenon is increasing the probability of a currency crisis once again, the new century is unlikely to play out the way the 1970s did because of debt.

When the seventies ended, Americans owed a small fraction of what they owe today. We were a net lender to the world. Even without including the tens of trillions in unfunded liabilities that the federal government owes, total American debt today is 49 trillion dollars, which is more than three times the size of our GDP, a level last approached when thousands of banks were collapsing in the 1930s. Families in the '70s saved an average eight percent of their take-home pay compared with virtually zero today. And after the deepest, longest property boom in our history it is becoming clear that real estate might not be participating in a real asset bull market, if currencies start to fall rapidly. To do so, Americans would need to take on even more credit and, as we have seen, our wallets are stretched like never before and banks are beginning to tighten lending standards. In fact, I think the problems emerging in real estate, which are closely tied to debt, could be the prime catalyst for a dollar collapse.

Part Two

OUR HOMES: THE EPICENTER OF AMERICAN ECONOMIC RISK

Chapter 5

Real Estate, this Decade's Economic Driver, Could Drive Us into Recession

We are not in a recession and yet the median home price is falling for the first time since the Great Depression, according to the National Association of Realtors.[1] This signals the end of perhaps the broadest, longest real estate boom in U.S. history, which began in 1991. As Figure 5.1 shows, the number of homes sold has been falling sharply, and house prices are flat or falling in a majority of American cities. However, the official house price indices are misleading since they are based only on homes actually sold, many of which are probably in markets with rising inventories of properties for sale.[2] For instance, in the once high-flying San Francisco Bay Area, home prices remained relatively flat in early 2007, but the number of homes sold in

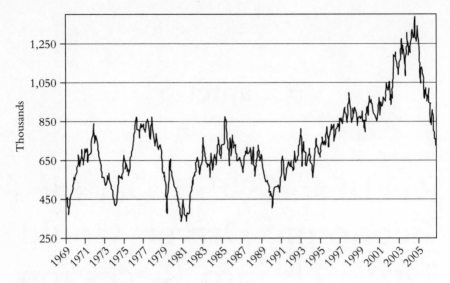

Figure 5.1 New Home Sales (in thousands)
SOURCE: U.S. Census Bureau.

March of that year were down a deep 20 percent compared with 2006.
Yet, mortgage default notices surged by 160 percent.[3] While there are a
few regions where residential real estate values are rising as I write in
2007, there is little doubt that homes in many areas across the country
are worth substantially less than they were a year or two ago based on
present market conditions.

While disagreeing about anything from interest rates, to inflation, to
the effect of Chinese outsourcing on American salaries, economists tend
to share this view: The continuing health of the U.S. economy is deeply
dependent on real estate. It has been the most important creator of jobs
in this decade. Americans have invested more in their homes—and
extracted more money from them—than ever before, and we close our
wallets more tightly during a housing bust than in the wake of a stock
market crash. Real estate is valued at a massive $22 trillion compared
with the $12 trillion that Americans held on their balance sheets before
the stock market crashed in 2000–2001.[4] With consumption accounting
for approximately 70 percent of U.S. gross domestic product—and a
fifth of global GDP—an intensifying of the present real estate crunch
would practically ensure a recession. In the months leading into the fall

of 2007, I attended meetings, heard conference calls, and read the research of many of the world's leading economists and each one often began his or her speech or paragraph by addressing American real estate. The news is not good.

Realtors are no longer singing the home-prices-never-go-down tune as the deepest credit-driven real estate boom the country has ever experienced is rapidly unraveling. Since the start of 2007, more than 40,000 workers have lost their jobs at mortgage lending institutions, according to company layoff announcements and data complied by global outplacement firm Challenger, Gray & Christmas Inc.[5] A Merrill Lynch analyst made a shocking suggestion in August: Countrywide Financial Corp., the nation's largest lender, could possibly go bankrupt due to liquidity problems in the real estate industry. This news is perplexing because we are not in a recession, and perhaps for the first time home prices have begun to weaken at a time when unemployment is falling and the economy expanding.

In the usual economic cycle, weaker profits nationwide prompt companies to lay off workers, which leads to a slackening of consumer spending and rising foreclosures, causing construction and real estate activity to eventually slow down. But now, the process is working in reverse as housing has *caused* a significant slowdown for the economy as a whole. In 2005, housing-related activity accounted for 23 percent of gross domestic product, according to Harvard's Joint Center for Housing Studies, and the slowdown had a significant effect on growth in the last year.[6]

Close to 40 percent of all private sector jobs created during the boom that began in 2001 were tied to the real estate industry.[7] With new and existing home sales falling 10 percent in 2006—and a deeper fall expected in 2007—more than 50 subprime real estate companies have already ceased operations, overwhelmed by non-payment and foreclosures across the country.[8] Slower orders have caused layoffs at companies like Whirlpool (refrigerators for homes), Masco (faucets), and many furniture makers.[9] The CEO of General Motors, whose more than $200 billion in total sales account for two percent of our GDP, announced in April 2007 that the mortgage "meltdown" had hit auto sales and, as Figure 5.2 shows, a clear downward trend in cars purchased nationwide has begun, this despite the continuing onslaught of no-down-payment and no-interest incentives.[10]

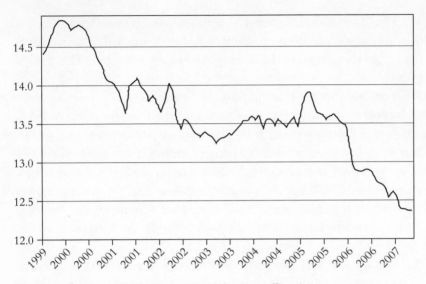

Figure 5.2 Annual Domestic Auto Sales (in millions)
Source: Bloomberg.

Though bad weather was partly to blame, retail chain store sales fell 2.4 percent in April 2007, the deepest drop since the International Council of Shopping Centers began tracking sales in 1970, driven primarily by "anything that is home-related."[11] Ecommerce sales growth in that month dropped to a level last seen in the weeks after the 9/11.[12]

The aggregate value of American houses rose almost 200 percent since 1991, and their values shot up by close to 50 percent between 2000 and 2005.[13] And, of course, prices doubled and almost tripled in several cities across the country in the last decade. For the level of home sales and prices to revert to the mean—that is, to go back to long-term trend levels of steady, gradual appreciation—they would have to fall pretty sharply. Even with the weakness we have been seeing, the number of new homes sold in 2006 was still well above the 40-year average—about 30 percent higher. At six percent of the economy, investment in residential construction was at a 50-year high in 2006. National home prices have been rising several times faster than family incomes since 1991. This is an anomaly unmatched in the history of modern real estate, and with the 15-year boom ending, what many see as a five-year bubble could take several years to decompress.

Despite the speed with which real estate activity and home price increases have decelerated, so far the dramatic rises in mortgage delinquency and foreclosures have been concentrated in subprime and so-called Alt A mortgages (which rank somewhere between prime and subprime in terms of risk for lenders). This explains why the economy has stayed fairly healthy. Though slowing rapidly, consumer spending remains positive, the unemployment rate is still quite low and there are even signs of a labor shortage in parts of the economy. Help wanted signs are common at the doors of fast food restaurants and retailers in Austin, Texas, which is one of the few cities that remains in a real estate boom. Perhaps most encouraging is that income growth has remained steady, the major factor that has reassured some economists and led them to predict that there will be no recession.

To calculate the probability that we might be going into a real estate-driven recession, statistically economists have very little to go by in terms of data. To reach a conclusion such as, "there is a 60% probability that home prices will fall 15% before this slowdown is over," one needs a minimum number of bad years to make any valid calculation. Maybe if we could find five bad periods we would have an acceptable statistical universe. But—with due respect to the countless PhDs in economics burning the midnight oil to forecast a further decline or recovery—we really have little to guide us for one simple reason. Despite sharp declines in many parts of the country over the years, the median national home price, as the army of real estate cheerleaders never tire of telling us, has not fallen in a single year for many decades.

But national home prices fell 2.7 percent in the fourth quarter of 2006, which was the biggest year-over-year drop on record, according to the National Association of Realtors.[14] And 2007 is expected to be even worse. Even with a few notable dips, like the early '80s recession and the subsequent Savings & Loan crisis, the median national home price has not fallen since 1930s.[15] Home values have risen eightfold since the late 1960s and there is little information about the real estate market for the years before then. We would really have to go back to the Great Depression, when the boom and bust first hit in (where else?) Florida and Charles Ponzi was making a name for himself, to read about a severe housing crunch.

I believe we are lacking periods with which to compare our present situation because in our lifetimes we have never seen 1) the scale and speed with which home prices increased; 2) the amount of lending provided and Americans' willingness to assume large debts to acquire property; 3) the availability of non-traditional, risky, and borderline unethical mortgage products (like the kind that make your mortgage balance go up!); and 4) the ease with which homes were made available to those who would not have qualified a decade ago—like the ones in recent years who didn't make a single payment from day one.

Considering that to sign an apartment lease one generally needs a month's deposit, it has been easier to buy a house ("It's zero move in week at Happiness Homes!") than rent perhaps for the first time in U.S. history. The consequences of risky mortgage lending are already clear: in 2006 home buyers putting up less than a five percent down payment represented almost half of all home purchases, implying (due to selling costs of at least six percent) that most of the new owners have negative equity today. Low documentation loans—better known as liar loans— accounted for 49 percent of purchase loans, almost triple the level of 2001.[16] Zero-down mortgages, the 125 percent home equity loan, inter- est-only financing, mortgage hybrids, negative amortization, double and triple loans on a single asset, no proof of income loans, more than two trillion dollars in equity extracted from real estate—These debt- enlarging concepts are new to the American home buyer, common as they now seem.[17]

But the mortgage industry, finally under pressure from slow-to-react regulators, is beginning to tighten lending standards, and many who would have qualified for zero-down, interest-only or option ARMs months ago are now being turned away, weakening demand for the climbing number of homes on the market even further. (See Figure 5.3.)

Long term interest rates have fallen only slightly, as the Fed remains concerned about inflation. But even if, out of concern about the real estate market, the Fed cut rates even further, this would likely have a minor effect on home lending since mortgage rates remain near multi- decade lows. They are unlikely to fall much further. And now that there are many high end residential real estate markets that are experiencing significant price declines, it can no longer be claimed that the housing crunch is solely affecting the real estate market's low end.[18]

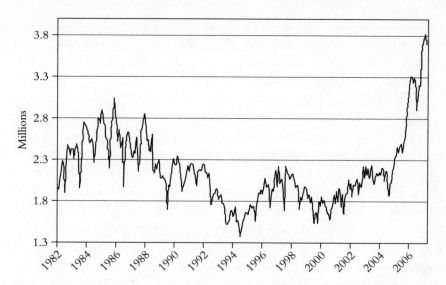

Figure 5.3   Total Existing Homes for Sale (in millions)
SOURCE: National Association of Realtors.

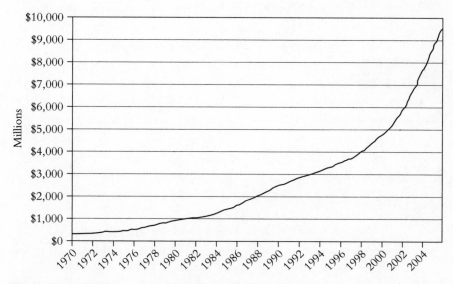

Figure 5.4   Total American Mortgage Debt (in millions)
SOURCE: Federal Reserve.

Like other observers, I believed this real estate boom was a bubble with a delayed pop, one that will take years to recover from and which is likely to lead the United States into a recession. As Merrill Lynch economist David Rosenberg has pointed out, our real estate problem resembles boom and bust cycles described by MIT Professor Charles Kindleberger in *Manias, Panics and Crashes*, though we are in an early stage of the downswing. Like all financial bubbles, the real estate boom and bust has been intimately tied with an unprecedented surge in credit because, absent the $4.7 trillion added in this decade—a doubling of American mortgage debt in six years—Americans would not have been able to buy and sell as much as we did. Homes grew less and less affordable across the country because prices were outpacing our salaries by a wide margin and we relied on credit—trillions and trillions of it—to make up the difference. Now that banks are scaling back their residential mortgage lending due to regulatory pressure, concerns about surging foreclosures and the sudden threat of lawsuits, it is reasonable to expect that the symptoms of withdrawal will be harsh on the American economy. (See Figure 5.4.)

Chapter 6

The Negative Amortization Mortgage Loan Is Born

Before the Fed decided to supply our economy with the biggest injection of monetary stimulus in history, which led to the deepest credit boom our financial system has ever experienced, home prices had generally appreciated in line with family incomes. This tendency to move in the same direction made sense because of the way in which banks offered mortgage loans. Although zero-down loans—which represented more than 40 percent of the loans offered in 2006—have been available for many years, these had generally been a small part of the mortgage loans written each year. Most of the non-commercial mortgages available to a typical family before recent years were traditional fixed-rate, amortizing loans that required a minimum down payment of 10 to 20 percent. And home buyers were generally not allowed to take out an additional loan to cover a down payment, as can be done today. Also, up until recent years banks were generally careful to ensure that the mortgage payment represented less than a third of the family's monthly income, long a rule of thumb in mortgage lending. Even if a client was expecting a big raise or planning to sell the house for a big profit, banks' lending rules generally would not allow mortgage payments to represent too large a part of a person's earnings. Since families could only borrow for a home based on the size of their incomes, it follows that home prices tended to rise with American salaries over time.

However, these traditional rules of thumb began to fly out the window when the banking industry found itself able to lend trillions in new funds thanks to the Federal Reserve. Fearful of a deep economic slowdown following the 2000 stock market crash and the 9/11 attack, the Fed began slashing the Fed Funds rate (the rate at which banks lend to one another) and ultimately drove down the rate and maintained it below inflation for three long years, which consequently permitted banks to offer borrowers the lowest interest rates in modern history. Turbo-charging the economy with negative real interest rates, which discouraged savings (since one earns negative inflation-adjusted interest), companies and individuals were able to restructure their debts and lower interest payments. But abundant credit helped many go a step further since it allowed them to assume risks they couldn't take under normal circumstances. And the financial industry itself, being able to borrow at rock-bottom rates, had more to lend than it knew what to do with. I remember reading in the summer of 2004, when the real estate boom was fast approaching its peak, that banks had three trillion dollars in unused consumer credit lines available.[1] This despite having mailed roughly four billion credit offers to Americans the year before.[2]

For many years, banks have sold part of their mortgage loan portfolios to mortgage giants Fannie Mae and Freddie Mac, government-sponsored enterprises that in turn sell mortgage-backed bonds, thereby freeing up part of banks' capital to be used for further lending. In 1990, close to 40 percent of mortgages issued by banks were being converted into bonds.[3] However, over time banks have learned how to securitize, that is to bundle other mortgages and types of consumer loans—anything from credit card receivables to mobile home mortgages—into mortgage- or asset-backed, often tradable, securities. These are sold in turn to institutional investors, such as fixed income funds, insurance companies, pension funds, hedge funds, and foreign investors. In purchasing hundreds of billions in mortgage-backed securities from banks in recent years, these institutions have effectively become banks to the banks.

Up until a credit crunch suddenly hit debt markets in the summer of 2007, 80 percent of mortgages were being converted into bonds, which allowed banks to free up even more capital, spreading their lending risks among more investors. There had been plenty of so-called "appetite" for these high-yielding debt securities.[4] In fact, foreign investors have become the fastest-growing source of demand for banks' mortgage- and asset-backed securities, and as a result it is becoming more and more likely that the funds borrowed to purchase a home or refinance a mortgage in the United States are ultimately coming from outside the country.[5] A large part of this external funding is from foreign central banks, which are trying to gain a greater return on their fast-rising dollar reserves than that provided by the U.S. Treasury securities they traditionally invested in.

In addition to having more capital freed up due to securitization and lower interest rates, the lending industry was prepared for the boom in other ways. The Internet facilitated rapid-fire loan approvals and several versions of automated mortgage loan underwriting software were already in widespread use in 2001, a boon to the growing number of mortgage brokers that helped home buyers surf the Web for the best deal. New Century Financial, the second largest subprime lender in the country before it went belly-up early in 2007, used a FastQual automated system. "We'll give your loan answers in just 12 seconds!" it used to advertise brazenly.[6] Automated underwriting, which saves customers and lenders time, reduced closing costs for financial companies by an average of $916, according to a 2001 Fannie Mae survey.[7] But the more than 3,000 risk variables that some underwriting programs used to weed out risky borrowers and welcome the credit-worthy must have had a bug. Because the *majority* of the country's subprime lenders, many of which relied on these systems, have gone out of business since the beginning of 2006.[8]

In addition to competing on speed of mortgage loan approval, lenders had to deliver what was vital to most home buyers: finding the lowest monthly payment. As home prices across the nation began to skyrocket and rampant speculation was unleashed—not only by first time home buyers, but by second- and third-home buyers and investors of many stripes—supply quickly hit the wall. This happened first in cities where it was most constrained, on the East and West coasts, and then in other areas of the country. Despite booming home prices, demand was still increasing and affordability fell through the floor because salaries were not keeping pace. By mid-2005, only 18 percent of California households could afford to buy a median-price house using a conventional fixed rate mortgage. Not surprisingly, by that time the Mortgage Bankers Association had revealed that more than half of national mortgage originations were adjustable-rate and interest-only mortgages.[9]

These mortgage products, which have offered borrowers the advantage of a low initial mortgage payment that can be 20 percent lower than that of a traditional amortizing loan, were a key driver of mortgage demand in this decade. Interest-only mortgages allow borrowers to defer payment of principal for several years, while option-adjustable rate mortgages (also called pick-a-payment mortgages) go so far as permitting a home buyer to pick among several payment structures each month—a higher debt-amortizing payment, an interest-only option, or an even lower payment that actually increases the loan principal balance. But now, with home sales and prices sagging, these non-traditional mortgages are increasingly being called simply "negative amortization" loans, as that is what they have become for many Americans—money-sucking financial instruments that *reduce* home equity. Since the multiple pay-less-now-and-more-later mortgage variations simply postpone the payment or loan principal, they effectively increase or delay paying down a borrower's debt much like a credit card, where principal accumulates, making the total debt more burdensome. This has become a problem in many cities, like San Francisco, where 28 percent of 2005 mortgage originations were negative amortization loans—about ten times the level seen in 2002.[10] But low initial payment loans are now a national phenomenon to which regulators are finally paying attention.

Chapter 7

Tighter Lending Standards and the Fed Can't Help

During a speech in late 2005, Comptroller of the Currency John Dugan, the country's most important banking system regulator, said this to a gathering of national mortgage lending experts:

It seems like only yesterday when a 5/1 ARM was considered a risky mortgage product. And it was—but primarily for borrowers, who, in return for lower initial payments, assumed the interest rate risk that had previously been borne by lenders. Today's non-traditional mortgage products—interest-only, payment option ARMs, no doc and low-doc, and piggyback mortgages, to name the most prominent examples—are a different species of product, with novel and potentially risky features. I don't have to explain those features to you,

because these products have come to dominate the mortgage originations that many of you look at every day.

He went on to list his concerns about widespread use of the new
mortgages, such as the "payment shock" that may be awaiting interest-
only borrowers in the years ahead. He also discussed the "layering of
multiple risks" in the mortgage market as several risky features were
often being combined into a single loan: "The total risk is greater than
the sum of the parts."[1]

Dugan was concerned that American banks in late 2005 appeared to
have reached the top of the credit cycle, which is when problems tend
to appear. Whereas in 1990, less than 3 percent of homebuyers made down
payments of less than 5 percent, that percentage had increased six-fold to
17 percent by 2005. Forty-three percent of first-time purchasers bought
homes with no money down in that year, and about half of all mortgages
being offered were either piggybank or lower-documentation loans.[2]
Perhaps most alarming to regulators is that adjustable-rate and interest-only
mortgages, some of the riskiest loans for homebuyers, were most prevalent
in areas of the country where average home prices were highest. For
instance, close to 66 percent of all 2005 homebuyers in the Washington D.C.
area used interest-only or option mortgages, compared to a mere 2.2 percent
in 2000.[3]

In 2005, mortgage lenders were actually reducing their lending standards even further, by dropping the minimum credit score required of
borrowers, lowering down payment requirements and becoming even
more lenient regarding documentation of income and assets.[4] But this
began to change in 2006, as banks responded to the sudden rise in delinquency and foreclosures as well as increasing regulatory warnings, such the
one from John Reich, director of the Office of Thrift Supervision. Speaking to the New York Bankers Association, he said regulators were "closely
monitoring" the growth of loan products in which payments can suddenly
double, causing a payment shock that could intensify the risk of foreclosure.
He stated that regulators were drafting a specific warning for the industry
that could restrict the use of such loans.[5]

Now that the subprime credit crunch has exploded into a disaster that
even the most pessimistic observers had not anticipated, "it's going to be
very difficult, if not impossible, to do a no-money-down loan at any credit

score," said Alex Gemici, president of the New Jersey-based mortgage bank Montgomery Mortgage Capital Corp.[6] Since so many homebuyers in recent years have relied on zero-down and low initial-payment mortgage financing, it remains to be seen how deep an effect a sharp reduction in these products' availability will have. Some are expecting the impact to be severe. "These products have been enablers when it comes to allowing home prices to rise," said Christopher Cruise, a Washington D.C.-based mortgage trainer who offers classes for lenders and regulators around the country. Without them, "homes couldn't be purchased. If they are taken off the market, it could precipitate a disaster of epic proportions."[7]

Subprime and so-called Alt-A mortgages together represented almost 40 percent of all mortgage loans being offered in early 2007. Credit Suisse mortgage expert Ivy Zelman believes tighter lending standards could slash subprime mortgages in half in 2007 and Alt-A mortgages by around a quarter, which is likely to have a deep effect on mortgage demand throughout the market. First-time home buyers are often subprime borrowers with weak credit, but their purchases are vital to the real estate chain. As one real estate expert put it, "The buyer of a $300,000 house enables the seller of that home to buy a $450,000 house, and up the line until you get to a luxury home. None of that happens unless the first-time buyer makes the purchase."[8]

Banks are tightening their mortgage lending standards at an accelerating pace now that foreclosures are surging across the country. Once restricted to high-riding California and Florida, now states like Idaho and Oregon, not to mention Vermont and Colorado, are also reporting a steep drop in sales and rising inventories of homes on the market.[9] Giving up on selling foreclosed properties via real estate agents, some banks have resorted to auctions lately, and the results have been alarming in several cases. At a San Diego sale in May 2007, houses and condos typically sold for 30 percent below their previous sale or appraisal prices, and the discounts reached nearly 50 percent for some properties.[10]

Unfortunately, help from the Fed does not appear to be on the way. Many of the riskier types of mortgages are tied to short term rates, which rose more than four percentage points since the low of one percent in 2003. But inflation has remained uncomfortably high, and the Fed appears reluctant to cut rates deeply. Perhaps, considering the dollar's persistent weakness, Fed governors are also aware of the weakening effect further rate cuts would have on our currency, a factor that could lead to higher inflation down the road. Of equal importance is the fact that long-term interest rates, which are closely tied to mortgage rates, remain near a multi-decade low. Both the U.S. Treasury 10-year and 30-year bonds are yielding less than five percent, one of the lowest points in the history of bonds. (See Figure 7.1.) If yields start to fall even further, this could actually be a sign of deep problems. Yields that are too low can be a signal of the deflationary risks the Fed was deeply concerned about in 2003, and banks might not necessarily begin reducing mortgage rates now that real estate risk is surging.

With the great many low payment options available for years, thanks to banks' lax lending standards as well as the negative real interest-rate environment provided by the Fed, just how far would interest rates have to fall for them to have a salutary effect on the real estate market? Perhaps, as Bill Gross, the director of Pimco, the world's largest bond fund manager, pointed out in April, the best way to answer this is to look at housing affordability.[11] Considering that 2003 was perhaps the last year in which home price appreciation levels were "normal," according to

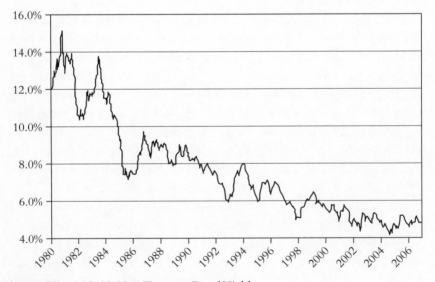

Figure 7.1 U.S. 30-Year Treasury Bond Yield
SOURCE: Bloomberg.

Yale professor and real estate expert Robert Shiller, home prices are perhaps 15 to 20 percent overvalued.[12] If home prices don't come down to make them more affordable to buyers, mortgage rates might have to come down as much as a full percentage point. But as Figure 7.1 implies, that seems highly unlikely. Home prices are probably going to have to come down by themselves, perhaps very sharply.

Chapter 8

The Great American Equity Cash-Out Is Coming to an End

O n August 31, 2004, I, and perhaps some of the persons reading
this book, received this email message:

LendingTree is pleased to present you with another way to help
you gain control of your finances.

Smart Borrower Tip: No Equity? You can still get a Home
Equity Loan or Line of Credit. Even if you have little or no equity
in your home, LendingTree can help you get a home equity loan
or line of credit. Many LendingTree Lenders Offer up to 125%
of Your Home's Value.

- Rates as low as 3.99%
- Consolidate debt
- Make home improvements
- Finance nearly any expense

I think nothing reflects the changes in our financial culture more than mortgage equity withdrawal (MEW), what Morgan Stanley economist Gerard Minack called the "residential ATM" phenomenon. Thanks to an extremely simple transaction that often takes less than an hour at the bank and a few days for final approval, Americans have been able to extract roughly $2.8 trillion dollars from their estimated house values since the real estate boom began, according to a measure designed by former Fed Chairman Alan Greenspan and Fed economist Jim Kennedy.[1] While a sharp drop in interest rates beginning in 2001 helped many homeowners refinance mortgage loans into ones that required lower payments, in recent years Americans mainly have been using refis to raise cash by increasing their debts. Nine out of 10 homeowners who refinanced in the second quarter of 2006 cashed out additional equity, which, given higher interest rates, implies that they increased debt at an average half-percentage point higher interest rate than the rate of the previous year.[2] So, many home-owners were taking on more mortgage debt at higher interest rates near what appears to have been the peak of the biggest real estate boom ever. (See Figure 8.1.)

The economic impact of MEW has been enormous since home-owners have been able to maintain high consumption levels even when American wages were stagnating. Economist Gene Sperling, pointing to the connection, said that inflation-adjusted wages did not gain a penny between November 2001 and August 2006, and yet consumption grew at a healthy 3.2 percent between 2002 and 2006.[3] Goldman Sachs and the IMF both estimated that home-equity extraction dollars have certainly been making their way into spending in recent years, with Goldman estimating that consumers were spending 50 cents of each dollar extracted, and the IMF a more modest 18 cents.[4]

Before the present real estate boom took flight in recent years and MEW began to rise into the hundreds of billions each year, home equity extraction tended to be a rarity for most households, something to resort to in an emergency. In fact, before 2001 residential real estate equity withdrawal was

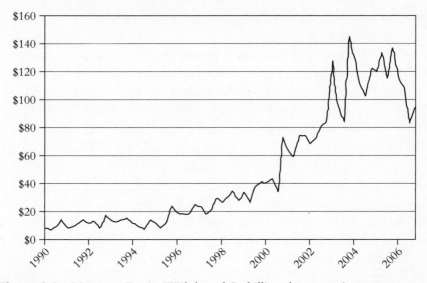

Figure 8.1   Mortgage Equity Withdrawal (in billions by quarter)
SOURCE: Federal Reserve.

often negative because many Americans were paying down mortgage debt more quickly than they needed to. Many families were evidently adding a little more to each monthly mortgage check or even making 13 payments a year, so that they could be debt-free on their homes sooner.

Today, even after the biggest surge in home values we have ever seen in a five-year period, American equity as a percentage of our home values is at an all-time low of 52.7 percent, thanks largely to equity extraction.[5] And this percentage will evidently fall further now that house prices are falling. Although booming prices have driven the total dollar value of home equity to a record high, most of the 2006 new home buyers have negative equity today. A large portion of them did not make a down payment and among those that put money on the table, the average down payment was at a record low. Since home owners typically spend anywhere from six to 10 percent of their home values in selling costs—not counting any discounts necessary to offload a house in a tough market—a great many low equity homeowners are upside-down on their mortgage loans today. Considering the high level of home inventories for sale in many areas of the country—particularly in those where the boom was strongest—home prices might not have fallen even further because many low equity home sellers simply cannot bring their selling prices down.

Overall American home equity appears healthy on paper at a massive $12 trillion, according to Federal Reserve estimates. However, as the boom began to end in March 2006, mortgage debt was beginning to grow faster than home prices, and continued into 2007, which implies that American home equity continues to go down as a percentage of the value of homes. The unprecedented trillions of dollars extracted have reduced the wealth that many Americans have in their homes, while increasing overall debt and mortgage payments as a percentage of income to record levels.

The high value of homes, much like the high value of any asset that can be bought and sold in a free market, is dependent on the degree of buying interest. If I had a Rolls Royce appraised at $200,000, but needed to sell it in a hurry and could find zero buyers amidst a glut of similar vehicles on the market, how much would my car really be worth? Unlike the price of IBM, the Internet and newspapers cannot list the actual value of your car or home. You only find out when someone else is willing to write a check. And if my Rolls only got a $100,000 bid, that would be its value at this point in time.

The United States is coming off the biggest home-buying bonanza the country has ever lived through, and a great many of us were willing to incur all the costs implied in owning a home because we believed in the continuing rapid appreciation in real estate values.[6] But this has changed now that national home values have fallen for the first time since record-keeping began decades ago, and the National Association of Realtors is predicting that they will fall further.[7] A new house, in addition to giving rise to those further expenses, is not something that one can sell quickly or easily. It can be far riskier than investing in the stock market, a fact that may begin to change many minds about the wisdom of seeing our homes as an investment.

Chapter 9

Financial Culture Shock: Real Estate Can Have a Negative Return

In 2004, well into the real estate boom, one in four homes bought was purchased for investment purposes and 13 percent as vacation homes.[1] This means that more than a third of all homes sold in the United States were second homes, and the trend continued into 2005 and 2006. Coming off the back of a deep stock market disappointment a few years before, the amazing investment drive into real estate made sense to a great many of us—even those who did not earn enough to borrow large amounts, since we could lie about our incomes and pile into more than one real estate venture, often securing a condo with a simple letter of credit.[2] Optimism was higher than ever; there was no housing bubble, most believed, and condoflip.com made the prevailing sentiment clear with its banner: "Bubbles are for bathtubs."

Homebuyers surveyed in 2003 were expecting average home prices to rise at a double-digit percentage pace over the following ten years. Milwaukee homebuyers expected an average home price appreciation of 11.7 percent per year for the next decade, while those in San Francisco anticipated a stunning 15.7 percent rise in each year, well above the most optimistic expectations for the stock market.[3] Even those not buying were participating in the real estate boom by extracting equity from their homes. In 2003, the average line of credit being used was $69,500, up significantly from $55,000 the previous year, and on average homeowners were tapping those lines 3.7 times a year, taking out $13,142 on each occasion.[4]

It was rational, the prevailing wisdom at the time dictated, to cash equity out of homes and invest it, to borrow at ease below six percent to make a super-return on something else. And surveys from boom times show that most of those doing so were increasing debt to invest further in real estate.[5] While a large number of respondents said part of cash-out proceeds went toward paying off other forms of debt, like what was owed on credit cards ("consolidation" sounds better), in 2003 most proceeds went toward home improvements, like room additions or new kitchens, although some also went toward autos and household appliances. The investment logic for the 2000s appeared to be: The stock market is uncertain, but reinvesting in my home makes sense as real estate values are rising, and I get to enjoy the newly added TV room, anyway. This logic helped ease the guilt that might accompany borrowing $40,000 to spend on the in-ground pool or add-on apartment. We tried to justify home improvement expenses as an investment, implying that there would be a net positive return.

Unfortunately, the numbers just don't add up—even when home prices are rising.

Generally, homeowners get back 70 to 80 cents on each dollar spent to add a bathroom or family room or remodel a kitchen; hence, a negative return, a losing investment. The $40,000 invested is likely to become less than $32,000, and yet the mortgage payment—not to mention higher utility bills, maintenance and repair costs, and perhaps taxes—would rise due to the equity cash-out.[6] The impact is worse if a home is sold shortly after an improvement. Chris Mayer, director of Columbia University's Milstein Center for Real Estate, said in 2004 that for many investments "the return is 50 cents on the dollar if you sell soon after making the improvements."[7] With such paltry returns on improvement investment, the tax shield derived from mortgage interest deduction becomes a cruel joke. The justification then might be "Well, but I get to enjoy it." But that's the point: Home improvements are generally a losing financial investment; they are really an investment in our present happiness, which of course has a positive return, albeit not a monetary one. Withdrawing equity and reinvesting it into our homes generally reduces our wealth.

An investment that requires regular payments of interest and principal running into the thousands of dollars, as well as cash disbursements to cover property taxes, insurance, maintenance, and repair costs, does not seem like much of an investment if its value is not going up rapidly. It looks even worse if it is not going up at all, or falling as is occurring with home prices in many part of the country today. Now that a record 70 percent of American households own their homes; now that so many have upsized to bigger houses and moved to better neighborhoods; now that a larger number of Americans than ever own second and third homes; and now that American mortgage debt is approaching $10 trillion, no doubt many will begin to wonder how wise it was to make real estate a bigger part of our overall wealth.

Should the home we live in really be considered an investment comparable to stocks and bonds? Although some markets have been stronger than others, national residential house prices have risen a mere 5.9 percent on average per year since 1963.[8] This is substantially worse than the stock market's performance, and more comparable to the returns of government bonds, which expose investors to substantially fewer risks than real estate.

Perhaps it is the realization that residential property can be a bad investment that is making the number of vacant homes for sale surge off the charts, a particularly worrisome development. (See Figure 9.1.) This is because a family living in a home wanting to sell it can postpone the decision in a bad market, while the seller of a second or third home might decide to leave it on the market, since he or she simply wants to get rid of the property— even at a deep loss—to avoid continuing to make mortgage payments on what has become a poor investment. This applies significant pressure on the rest of the market, and makes owners holding paper-thin equity particularly nervous.

Looking back a few years ago, when real estate prices were very strong, a great many investors seem to have made the discovery that the

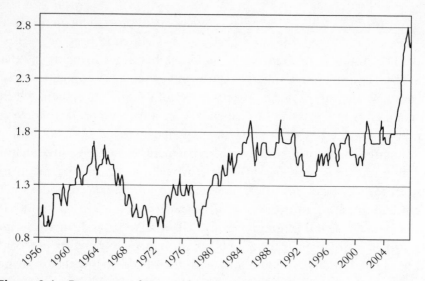

Figure 9.1   Percentage of Homes for Sale that Are Vacant
SOURCE: U.S. Census Bureau.

expected return on real estate was substantially higher than the eight percent that stocks can be expected to return in any given year. But it's not that expected returns on real estate suddenly became higher. They have always been higher—really. The expected rewards have been higher because property investment generally requires that you put up a large amount of money and sit on the investment for a long time—making payments each month—while the investment matures. Profitably flipping a property in a year—or two or three—is an extremely unusual event, not because prices can't go up fast enough (we know they can!), but because there are entry and exit fees that skim money off the top in buying and selling expenses. You can't pay four dollars a trade, you have the risk of a down market, and you need to make those mortgage payments . . . and pay property taxes and maintenance expenses, all of which subtract from expected return.

Of course, a great many Americans have become wealthy with real estate, but as with stocks, so much of their net investment return has depended on their entry and exit points. Buyers in the early 1990s were acquiring properties at the bottom of the cycle, and have probably made a killing even if they sold at 30 percent below present prices, particularly if they live in San Diego. Property renters know that their "rental yield"

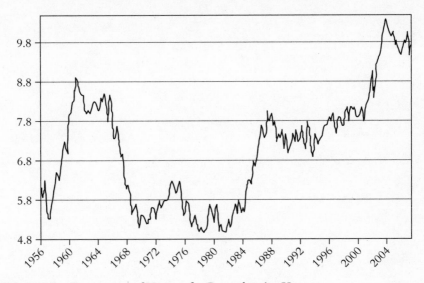

Figure 9.2   Percentage of Homes for Rent that Are Vacant
SOURCE: U.S. Census Bureau.

(the annual rent they receive divided by the value of the property being rented) is enhanced when the property is cheap. But today, rental yields in a great many markets are so low that it makes more sense to rent, a fact that is beginning to sink in as the real estate investment boom continues to implode. (See Figure 9.2.)

Part Three

OUR ECONOMY: THE LONGEST ECONOMIC BOOM EVER IS PROBABLY ENDING

Chapter 10

Balance Sheet Recession: We Could Be Heading in a Japanese Direction

One of the great myths of our time finds expression in the universal belief that no kind of economic activity should ever be inhibited by lack of money. The necessity to limit spending to the level of one's capacity to pay has been translated by experts to mean a "lack of liquidity," easily treated by the creation of credit.

W.P. HOGAN AND I.F. PEARCE,
THE INCREDIBLE EURODOLLAR (1982)[1]

In April 2007, a survey found that 60 percent of Americans expected a recession to begin within the next 12 months. A second survey in August, conducted by NBC and the *Wall Street Journal,* found that more than two-thirds of Americans thought a recession had already started or would begin the following year. These high percentages are reminiscent of the 64 percent of Americans who were anticipating an economic contraction in December 2000, on the eve of the 2001 recession—one virtually no economist was predicting.[2] Also in April 2007, perhaps not coincidentally, Michael Niemira, Chief Economist at the International Council of Shopping Centers, reported that April sales were the worst he had seen since he began tracking them in 1970.[3] First quarter economic growth dipped below one percent for the first time since the last recession, and the number of mortgages going into foreclosure rose to an all-time high.[4] And yet no Wall Street economist I know of, as I write in mid-2007, is predicting a recession, or even giving a significant economic slowdown any meaningful odds. The notable exception is Alan Greenspan, who rocked the stock market in February by suggesting economic contraction was a possibility.

There are important reasons economists remain optimistic about the future, despite the present slowdown. Inflation is manageable by historical standards, notwithstanding the growing price level concerns central bankers around the world have been expressing of late. Unemployment has remained low and wage growth has finally begun to pick up slightly after years of stagnation. European and Asian economies are booming, a factor driving our rising exports to the region, though overall exports remain substantially lower than our imports. Corporate America is flush with cash and, while companies are not investing enough (at least in the United States) to cause a significant employment boom such as we saw in the 1980s or '90s expansions—when the number of jobs being created was three to four times higher than today—corporate balance sheets are stronger than they were at the end of the '90s. Bad loans in the banking system remain low overall and liquidity, which we could regard as the ability to borrow easily, abundantly, and at low interest rates, remains plentiful.

The common denominator uniting much of this economic optimism is the perennial focus on growth. So long as corporate earnings are growing, consumers have jobs and are spending more, and the world economy is expanding rapidly, concerns can be put aside. I find the biggest irony in economists' focus on growth to be that what is growing most rapidly, by far, is mentioned the least: debt. No major economic variable is expanding faster. Not employment, much less wages, not business investment, not industrial production. According to Federal Reserve figures, federal government debt (not including the surging unfunded liabilities) jumped 45 percent state and local government debt 54 percent over the five years ending in 2006. Consumer debt rose 67 percent driven by $4.4 trillion in new mortgage credit, which helped the mortgage-backed securities market surpass the Treasury bond market in size for the first time.[5]

Much of the stock market's recent rise was caused by $460 billion in financing for corporate buyouts over the last five years, as well as close to $500 billion in levered loans—which is like saying indebted credits—to companies willing to pay higher rates.[6] American debt remains the ignored elephant in the room driving the U.S. economy, and until recently it had been doing so at an accelerating pace. Five dollars in debt are added for every dollar in GDP today, which means that we need more and more credit each day to continue growing. Being such a vital component of economic expansion, shouldn't we be concerned that the growth in debt, at least for consumers, is beginning to slow—and slow dramatically?[7]

In finance, analysts estimate any company's prospects for earnings growth alongside its ability to continue growing: They consider both the income statement and the balance sheet. As an example, AnyCompany's income statement subtracts what the company spends (wages, interest expenses, taxes, and other items) from what it earns in revenues derived from all that it produces to determine its net profit. AnyCompany is growing if revenues are rising faster than all its expenses. On the other hand, the company's balance sheet is a snapshot that shows the value of its assets and liabilities, the net difference being the equity or book value of the company.

Now, if AnyCompany's earnings were growing at a healthy pace, but the company's debt and related interest expenses were expanding more rapidly, at some point in time the company would face a problem: Profits would fall. To remedy this situation, creditors could refinance AnyCompany's debt by extending maturities, or by allowing it to postpone payments (with interest accruing), so that management could use the time to raise cash, or reduce expenses, or increase sales. But without a change, AnyCompany's rising debt would eventually cause earnings to fall because the expanding interest charges on that debt would overwhelm revenues and in time cause losses. Furthermore, the debt eating away at the balance sheet would cause Any-Company's equity to contract, as well. In time, the company would cease to operate and go into bankruptcy.

This logic can be extended to individuals, families, and countries. The United States has sustained a growing current account deficit—which could be seen as income statement losses—for many years and foreign creditors have allowed our debts to continue accumulating at a quickening pace to the detriment of our national balance sheet: In 1985, our net foreign assets (the difference between what we own and owe outside the country) turned to net foreign liabilities and the negative number is fast approaching three trillion dollars today. To meet rising expenditures—including interest payments on our $9 trillion national debt—Congress has raised the Federal Government's debt limit four times since 2000, and total federal liabilities have more than doubled in this decade.

As concerned analysts of this security called the United States, the world's economists understand that American deficits and the accumulating debt needed to support them cannot continue rising forever. Left unchanged, in time our annual interest charges—now $227 billion, twice what we spent in Iraq last year—would become larger than our gross domestic product.[8] But our stock, best represented by the dollar, hasn't crashed in part because our lenders and other participants in the global financial system understand that American leaders have options: Under pressure, the government can raise taxes, cut benefits, and lay off government workers. It can even turn to its last recourse, the Fed, which ultimately can print money to pay off public debt—an option that has been considered openly in Fed meetings.[9] The government can also buy time. So, going back to the company financial analysis analogy: The Federal government *can* continue to grow faster than its tax revenues despite the increasing threats to its solvency, at least for now. But what about its citizens?

American consumers, contributing more than a fifth of global GDP, are the single largest source of economic demand on the planet. Without our purchases of the world's oil and other commodities—cars, food, clothing, electronics—and the multiplicity of goods ranging from a few cents to millions in price, the world economy would be crippled. Every single one of the largest ten other world economies derives a significant portion of its GDP from exports to the United States. And over history, the effect of slowing consumption during U.S. recessions has generally led to economic contraction in countries like Germany, Japan, France, and Canada and today many emerging economies like China would no doubt be deeply affected by a slowdown.

Economists, much like analysts (as I have been), tend to be reactive instead of proactive, contemplative rather than predictive. We are a nation of optimists, of winners, and far more energy has been dedicated to forecasting why things will go up than to why they should fall. The going-down is generally an ex post facto explanation. The admired Yale economist Irving Fischer, who weeks before the greatest of all stock market crashes in 1929 made the memorably ill-fated comment that stock prices had "reached what looks like a permanently high plateau,", would be writing the classic "Debt-Deflation Theory of Great Depressions" just a few years later.[10] Nonetheless, for decades predicting doom has been a loser's game and the reason is clear. Financial markets tend to go up, as any long-term stock chart shows, and the odds the American consumer will throw in the towel in any given year are very slim. There are too many conspirators in their success. When selling less, retailers cut prices. Banks can offer loans on improved terms, refinance existing ones. The Fed can cut rates, the government taxes. And China can lend us hundreds of billions of dollars each year to keep American interest rates low so that we can afford to buy their products even if we have to borrow.

But what if interest rates on borrowing—having fallen for decades, as has occurred from 1981 to the present—stopped going down? What if banks, due to crippled balance sheets afflicted by a wave of foreclosures (like the ones arising today), finally began to close their doors to borrowers? What if taxes had been cut so deeply and so many times that some economists began to question the government's very solvency, as is the case today? What if consumer debt had doubled in seven years—quadrupled in the last twenty—and debt payments as a percentage of our disposable incomes had reached an all-time high—like today? What if people decided to start saving instead spending more than they earn each month, as we have been doing for years? Though our assets are worth more than ever, Americans have been *relying* on those assets—cashing them in, using our homes like ATM machines—to continue spending more than we earn in wages. Perhaps finally American consumers will begin focusing less on growth, and more on our neglected balance sheets.

"It looks like maybe the consumer, for the first time in my lifetime, might actually be tapped out," Steven Leuthold, the chief investment strategist for the financial company that carries his name, told *Barron's* this summer.[11] The main reason that he, and other economic observers have started to believe this, is that Americans have been in a cash flow deficit for several years. Figure 10.1 shows Americans' cash flow situation. The dip below zero indicates that we have been living off the value of our assets—mostly real estate—since the 2000 stock market crash to supplement

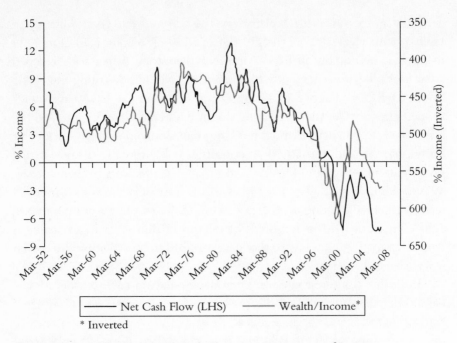

Figure 10.1 U.S. Household Cash Flow As a Percentage of Income
SOURCE: Morgan Stanley.

our incomes. Now that real estate prices are no longer rising and are widely expected to fall, that source of potential additional income has been slashed and proceeds from mortgage equity withdrawal, a significant source of economic growth in recent years, have simply collapsed. As banks continue tightening lending standards, as is widely expected, it will be harder to use our homes like ATM machines, as we have been doing over the last five years. Absent this additional source of income, the average American homeowner will have to tighten his or her belt.

Coming out of the Alan Greenspan era, a time when the Fed was often quick to cut interest rates at the earliest sign of a slowdown or financial turmoil, one would think our central bank will come to the rescue once again if consumers begin showing signs of stress. This is partly why the 2007 stock market often rallied on bad economic news: It could be the excuse the Fed needed to offer some financial relief via lower rates to the struggling housing market, and hence the overall economy. Excuses to cut short term interest rates and inject liquidity into the economy—meaning encouraging us to borrow—were rarely lacking over the nearly two decades that Greenspan presided over the institution, as Lawrence Meyer, a former governor of the Federal Reserve Board under the former chairman, made clear in a memoir. Throughout the book, *A Term at The Fed*, we find Greenspan's "disproportionate role in shaping monetary policy" to have influenced sometimes doubting members of the board to cut rates often and repeatedly at the sign of any trouble, be it the Asian Crisis, the Tequila Crisis, or Y2K, notwithstanding the effect lower rates were having on Americans' ballooning debt.[12]

In 2002, shortly after the stock market bubble (helped, no doubt, by low interest rates) had popped, the Federal Reserve began considering "unconventional policy options"—which among other things included cutting interest rates to virtually zero—to prevent a Japanese-style deflationary spiral, an economic calamity that was emerging as a distinct possibility at the time.[13] The objective of these unconventional options, which incidentally were being championed by current Fed Chairman Ben Bernanke, was to *maintain economic growth* (focus on the income statement) and prevent the decade of intermittent recessions Japan began suffering in 1990. Not much consideration was given to the condition of the American balance sheet—our ballooning debt.

What had happened in Japan that so worried the Fed? During the 1980s, Japan enjoyed the biggest credit-driven economic boom in its history. The poorly regulated banking system had lent freely in a speculative stock and property binge that eventually drove Japanese stock values to represent 42 percent of the total capitalization of the global stock market—three times the proportion it had represented just a decade earlier.[14] At its peak in 1990, the combined value of Japan's real estate had grown to five times the country's GDP, and roughly four times the value the total stock of property in the United States.[15] But the asset bubble began imploding sharply in 1990 with the Tokyo stock market crash and Japan rapidly moved into a period of deflation, as stock and property values collapsed and colossal debts remained: In the twelve years that ended in 1991, consumer debt had surged sevenfold to 67 trillion yen.[16] The Japanese economic descent that began in 1990 was the first experience with deflation that a major economy had suffered since the Great Depression. (See Figure 10.2.)

Figure 10.2   Japanese Inflation Remains Near Zero
SOURCE: Bloomberg.

Falling prices are not a trivial matter, as former Fed Governor Meyer explained:

> Deflation raises unique fears. First, we know how to end infla-
> tion: Raise interest rates. There's no limit to how high they can
> go, so there's no doubt that at some point you can end inflation.
> But how do you end deflation, especially if your policy rate hits
> zero and you have exhausted the ability to further stimulate the
> economy by conventional means…? This is exactly what hap-
> pened in Japan.[17]

But what Meyer did not mention is the effect of debt under deflation,
which is perhaps the more worrisome concern, particularly for economies
that are highly leveraged, like ours. During deflationary periods, asset values
(stocks, real estate, and other financial instruments) fall due to lower earnings on assets. Jobs are lost, and those who remain employed are often
forced to take wage cuts to allow companies to stay profitable. (This is what
is actually happening in the U.S. auto industry, where workers are being
forced to sacrifice benefits—and wages are not far behind.) But debt
remains unchanged. And since asset values decline, debt becomes a larger
burden on the balance sheet and individuals' net wealth falls.

During Japan's deflationary implosion in the 1990s, several American commentators repeatedly recommended that the Bank of Japan reduce interest rates even more deeply than it had already been doing to reactivate the depressed economy. The lower-rate medicine, so effective in the '80s and '90s U.S. economy, was prescribed in large part due to the influence of Milton Friedman and Anna J. Schwartz's *A Monetary History of the United States, 1876–1960*,[18] a classic that for decades was the standard history of the Depression for economics students.[19] In it, the authors lay much of the blame for our own terrible experience with deflation during the 1930s Great Depression—when the nation's GDP contracted by a third in just four years—on an ineffective Fed.

As thousands of banks began failing in the wake of the 1929 stock market crash, a collapse of commodity prices and a surge in mortgage foreclosures, the Fed "failed to exercise the responsibilities assigned to it in the Federal Reserve Act to provide liquidity to the banking system," Friedman and Schwartz claim.[20] As an important aside, it is worth mentioning that real estate loans and not failed stockbrokers' accounts—as myth has led us to believe to this day—were the largest single element in the failure of 4,800 banks in the 1930–33 period.[21] For Friedman and Schwartz, the early Fed—a "body of startling incompetence," as one economist called it—could have prevented a "normal," short-lived depression from turning into a catastrophe by lending more freely to banks, as is done at the shortest sign of trouble today.[22]

But Friedman and Schwartz's theory is, of course, "counterfactual," since it addresses what the Fed *could* have done, but without knowing if a much looser monetary policy and direct bank assistance actually would have mitigated effects of the Great Depression, as MIT economist Peter Temin has pointed out.[23] What if, due to the staggering size of debts in the 1930s, Americans had been unable or unwilling to take on *more* credit, even if terms improved? Their debts were actually rising relative to the declining value of their assets because inflation was falling. Consider what President Roosevelt wrote in 1933:

> In talking with people about our basic economic troubles I have often drawn for them a picture showing two columns—one representing what the United States was worth in terms of dollars and the other representing what the United States owed in terms of dollars. The figures covered all property and all debts, public,

corporate and individual. In 1929, the total of the assets in terms of dollars was much larger than the total of debts. But, by the spring of 1933, while the total of the debts was still just as great, the total of the assets had shrunk to below that of the debts.[24]

A Great Depression buff by his own admission, Fed Chairman Bernanke, in *Essays on the Great Depression*, discussed the "large and broad-based" expansion of debt in the 1920s economy, when three out of five cars and 80 percent of all radios were sold on installment credit, a financial novelty to the average American of that time—much like using homes as ATM machines is this century's innovation.[25] Growing at a snail's pace before the Fed began functioning in 1914, total debt in the U.S. economy rose a stunning 125 percent in the thirteen years ending in 1929—about half the speed of the credit expansion we've seen in this decade.[26] The 1920s United States had experienced an unprecedented surge in credit and when the hangover arrived Americans' revulsion toward debt, which drove so many families into bankruptcy, might have been such that no amount of easy credit would have changed their minds, strange as this is to imagine today.

This was the case in 1990s Japan, argues Nomura Chief Economist Richard Koo in *Balance Sheet Recession*, responding to American economists urging the Bank of Japan to slash interest rates.[27] Banks were "quite eager to lend," he explained, but businesses and individuals were saddled with excess liabilities and were "forced to pay down debts by curbing consumption and investment." The "last thing" they were interested in was *increasing* their liabilities. Writing in 2003, Koo said interest rates in Japan were at "the lowest ever recorded in human history," and yet demand for funds had remained subdued. Monetary policy had become totally ineffective since short term interest rates were reduced nearly to zero (and remain the lowest, by far, in the world today at half a percent).[28] Koo called Japan's predicament a "balance sheet recession," an economic quagmire so perplexing that Japanese authorities are still struggling to find a way back into a normal economy with some degree of inflation and healthy demand.

The main factor leading to a balance sheet recession is over-indebtedness—an inability on the part of consumers and the companies that depend on them to continue consuming at rates enjoyed in the past.

The Great Depression and Japan's recent years of deflationary stagnation are examples of such a recession, and policy-makers have been unable to find a precise remedy beyond the pain of actually paying down debt in a protracted economic standstill—or steep decline. The government—if it is not saddled with massive debt already, as ours is today—can only moderate economic pain by increasing its own spending, as President Roosevelt did in 1933 when he launched a protracted program of federal deficit spending. But if there is no pent-up demand because too much has been spent already and debt collectors are knocking on citizen doors, there can be no amount of fiscal or monetary stimulus sufficient to prevent a deep recession.

Going back to the Fed's deliberations in 2002, when its governors—encouraged by Bernanke—were considering "unconventional" monetary options to prevent the United States from falling into a Japanese-style balance sheet recession, the mission was clear: Reflate the economy—actually *create* inflation by encouraging Americans to continue spending—by keeping demand for the global economy's goods strong. Judging by the eventual bounce back in the world economy, and the strong growth seen in the last four years, one would think the Fed had been successful. Although corporate investment, a vital component of job creation and healthy economic growth, has remained subdued in the new decade, consumers are out shopping again, government spending is ever rising, and deflation, with all its terrible implications, has been avoided.

But was the Fed, in its zeal to reignite the American income statement (our economic growth) ignoring our balance sheets? Consumer debt rose by roughly one trillion dollars in each of the last five years, while wages for 80 percent of Americans have remained stagnant. Although the value of our assets, most notably our homes, was pumped up by the unprecedented easy access to credit, it remains to be seen just how healthy the demand necessary to maintain elevated property prices really is. For high house prices to remain steady, we need healthy consumer demand, which is already beginning to show significant signs of strain.

Deflation and balance sheet recessions are caused by debt levels that become so large as to be unmanageable for a large portion of the population. Spending less and trying to reduce leverage, individuals and families cause economic demand to contract, leading to retail price slashing, deep inventory reductions, and layoffs. What Irving Fisher called the "debt disease" leading to deflation is not something that can be .fought with lower interest rates, by encouraging the public to take on even more debt. We have already done that. Considering the debt boom the likes of which has not been experienced in the economic history of the United States, shouldn't economists finally begin to weigh the possibility of a balance sheet recession, terrible as that is to contemplate?

Chapter 11

Smiling on
the Lawnmower:
Affluent Poverty

Perhaps the most important question in global economics today is how to deal with the imbalances, a seemingly vague term whose troubling essence is clear to all macroeconomists. The world's largest economy consumes six percent more than it produces each year and to do so the United States depends on financing from the rest of the world. Most believe, as discussed in Chapter 3, that the financing side of this Bretton Woods II economic arrangement is not an immediate concern, as the world's central banks have given no sign they will stop lending vast amounts to the United States each year. China, Japan—and in recent years Russia and all other major economies—should continue propping up the dollar to keep their currencies weak and ensure their products and companies remain competitive in the global market. Since they need us to buy from them, vendor financing is safe for now, most agree.

So much for the lending side of what Morgan Stanley economist Stephen Roach regards as the "Reverse Marshall Plan." But what about the Americans spending the money side of the equation? Given our enduring desire as a nation to spend beyond what we earn each month—a degree of unbalanced consumption that only countries like Spain and Ireland, which have popping real estate bubbles of their own, can match—one could almost visualize a conspiracy theory explaining why our consumption never slowed after the devastating stock market crash of 2000 and the 9/11 terrorist attack, which many feared would force Americans to shut their wallets.

With Japan and Europe effectively remaining dormant economically, only Americans could be relied on to keep the world engine running fast after the stock market crash. But with dot-com dreams dashed and post the 9/11 attacks, we needed economic hope. So, no doubt remembering what occurred following the 1929 crash, when authorities reacted too slowly and prosperity ended in the Great Depression, the powers that be worked together to keep Americans consuming: With Alan Greenspan's blessing, our government passed the deepest tax cuts in American history, turning budget surpluses into deep deficits and more than doubling federal long-term liabilities; the Fed slashed interest rates faster and deeper than ever before and maintained extremely lax lending standards. Other central banks—preeminently China and Japan—lent us hundreds of billions of dollars each year via American bond purchases, which ensured the most encouraging credit environment our banks have ever offered. As Wall Street and the banking industry flooded the market with easy credit (benignly referred to as liquidity), everything from cheap Asian imports to furniture and cars could be had with little or no interest at all, and at times no payments for years. Most importantly, lower interest rates, poor regulation, and never seen exotic and borderline unethical mortgage loan products—like ones that make home equity go down—allowed more of us to buy and sell bigger and better houses, driving the deepest real estate bubble ever seen. Meanwhile, growing concerns about stagnant wages and skyrocketing consumer debt were alleviated by Greenspan and many Wall Street economists who offered statistics to show that Americans were actually wealthier than ever.

Conspiracy theories are usually flawed because the visualized Machiavellian ends tend not to add up—they call for the agreement of a large number of people (who are often not criminals) to do something wrong or unlawful. And thus the conspiracy described above would have required that our federal government, the Federal Reserve, and key global central bankers and government leaders knowingly agree to raise the financial risk of American citizens higher than ever for the sake of maintaining global economic growth. Obviously, this was not the case—at least the knowingly part—and yet something does not make sense. The lower interest rates, the tax cuts, and the lending deluge have made American families richer than ever, we are told, and yet there seem to be a lot of smiling guys riding around on lawnmowers these days.

I'm referring to the man in a TV commercial driving a sit-down lawn mower as he smilingly describes his ample assets—the cars, the home, the membership at the snazzy country club. "How could I afford all these things?" he asks the camera. "Because I am up to my eyeballs in debt!" It was an advertisement for a debt consolidation company, one of the many that appear on television these days, but I think he epitomizes a great many Americans today. Have we really gotten richer by borrowing more? "Maybe there is a free lunch," *Barron's'* Gene Epstein cheerfully wrote in 2007, explaining how it is possible that we are getting richer without saving. The way we measure savings is wrong, he and other economists say, and Federal Reserve figures back up the assertion.[1]

If we are richer than ever, why are foreclosures at an all-time high (and expected to rise much higher) when there is no recession, when unemployment is well below 5 percent?[2] This has never happened before. Why is the median home price falling for the first time since the Great Depression? Are the rapidly climbing number of uninsured families abandoning health benefits so that they can invest in the stock market? The Census Bureau reported that 47 million Americans—a new record—lacked health insurance in 2006. That's about one in six persons in the country and there are no visible signs that this ratio is improving.[3] A private study in 2007 found that only 66 percent of workers report that they or their spouse have any retirement savings at all, a new low.[4] Another one, based on nearly 200,000 workers that participate in 401(k) plans, found that nearly half of U.S. workers cash out of them completely when they change jobs. Too many workers are "using termination of employment as an opportunity to spend this money," the study's director said.[5] These are hardly the signs of a nation at the summit of its wealth.

Now, selectively picking alarming statistics is no way to make an economic argument, as the disappointed economists making dire predictions during the 1990s boom can attest to. And besides, it will take years before we have the data with which to reach any kind of solid economic conclusion about the present. But the depth of the credit explosion—American consumer debt doubled in less than a decade—coupled with stagnant wages for most workers should make us question the assertion that our nation is wealthier.

For example, the estimated value of residential real estate—where 33 percent of total American household assets reside—climbed 71 percent during the five years ending in the first quarter of 2006, the point at which home prices began to show signs of weakness. But mortgage debt, partly due to equity cash-outs running into the trillions, rose a larger 75 percent. In fact, a year later, mortgage debt was growing twice as fast as home prices.[6] If most American family wealth is in our homes, how can we be wealthier if mortgage debt has been climbing faster than house prices? The reason can be found in the Fed's quarterly Flow of Funds report, which shows that since financial markets have continued to perform well, our investments in checkable deposits, mutual funds, and other accounts continue to grow at a healthy pace. Hence, the Fed calculates that the net worth of U.S. households climbed to a massive $56 trillion at the end of the first quarter of 2007, notwithstanding weakening home prices.[7]

However, considering that much of what is keeping household wealth climbing is based on investments—as house prices have hit the rocks—the $56 trillion figure is likely being distorted by the top 10 percent of American families that have substantial investments in stocks, bonds, and alternative investments and have larger incomes. An academic study based on 2005 tax returns found that the top 1 percent of Americans—those with incomes above $348,000—earned their largest share of national income since 1928.[8] Between 1980 and 2005, an MIT study found that this richest 1percent of tax filers claimed 80 percent of all income gains between 1980 and 2005.[9] Although the combined income of all families rose 9 percent in 2005, income actually dropped for the bottom 90 percent of Americans, while that fortunate top 1 percent gained 14 percent.[10]

Data also showed that the top 300,000 Americans collectively earned as much as the bottom 150 million Americans.

While wealthy households are making substantial income and investment gains, they have also partaken in the great American debt binge. A Federal Reserve study found that the richest 1 percent of Americans had increased their debt *sevenfold* between 1998 and 2001, no doubt taking advantage of leveraged opportunities to amplify investment gains. But unlike their whale share of the nation's total wealth—33 percent—this group of high-net worth individuals only held 6 percent of all consumer debt in 2001, a proportion that is likely similar today. Meanwhile, the country's bottom 90 percent held only 30 percent of national wealth, yet more than 70 percent of the debt.[11]

This implies that the Federal Reserve's Flow of Funds report, which reflects the aggregate wealth of the nation, is inflated by successful Americans and flatters the picture we have of the bottom 90 percent of people that hold far more debt than they did just a few years ago—and about the same real incomes. In San Francisco, where the median home price is around $750,000, some houses were still being sold above the asking price in the summer of 2007, but in Atlanta, where the median price is less than half that level, some foreclosed houses were being auctioned off at 30 to 40 percent discounts.[12] New York City apartment prices, obviously well above the country's average, were still climbing, and yet the national foreclosure rate had reached an all-time high. If a great many families are beginning to lose their homes across the country, the widely-cited average wealth figure is likely being pushed up by the extremely affluent upper slice of the population.

Although it will take several years for economists to determine the extent of the dilemma, I believe there are a great many families living in what I call affluent poverty: rich in assets, heavily indebted, and yet poor in net wealth. The trillions in credit that Americans have used to acquire consumer goods, cars, furniture, and—most significantly—homes in recent years is likely to subtract from their ability to buy more in the future as they struggle to make payments. While obtaining credit has long been easy—at least up until mid-2007—the ability to acquire big ticket items without a down payment or any initial payment at all is surely unprecedented.

	Total Consumer Debt (billions)	Increase (YoY) $ (billions)	%	Debt/ Household	Increase (YoY) $	%
2Q 2007	$ 13,331	$ 982	8%	$ 121,191	$ 7,481	7%
2Q 2006	$ 12,349	$ 1,218	11%	$ 113,710	$ 9,877	10%
2Q 2005	$ 11,131	$ 1,112	11%	$ 103,833	$ 9,140	10%
2Q 2004	$ 10,019	$ 1,004	11%	$ 94,693	$ 8,351	10%
2Q 2003	$ 9,014	$ 941	12%	$ 86,342	$ 7,963	10%
2Q 2002	$ 8,073			$ 78,379		
Change Since Beginning of Decade		$ 6,917	107.8%		$ 58,921	95%

Figure 11.1 U.S. Consumer Debt

SOURCE: Federal Reserve, U.S. Dept. of Commerce, Bureau of Labor Statistics.

Consider that in 2006 it was still possible to buy a car, a boat and make many other significant purchases and then completely furnish and buy a home (remember "Zero Move-In!" ads?) without making a single payment. So, conceivably someone earning $50,000 a year could have taken on, say, $300,000 in debt in a week without making a payment based mostly on their past credit history and not their ability to pay for the new possessions. As two fund managers put it in an interview in *Barron's* not long ago, referring to our huge mortgage debt: the money has been spent, "it's already in the gross domestic product retrospectively. Prospectively, where is the money going to come from to pay the obligations that remain?"[13] (See Figure 11.1.)

Perhaps there is no better evidence for affluent poverty than the subprime mortgage *Titanic* that is submerging in slow motion. Surely the record number of families being forced to lose their homes in foreclosure are nowhere near the average family that supposedly has several hundred thousand dollars in net wealth.

As the Fed looked on, a great many people in that bottom 90 percent of income earners were seduced into buying that bigger, better house by 1 percent and 2 percent teaser rates and zero down. But now those 1- and 2-percenters are resetting into much higher rate mortgages causing a tsunami of foreclosures across the country, and perhaps the worst is yet to come. Bank of America estimates that close to $500 billion in adjustable rate mortgages will reset in 2007, and another $700 billion in 2008.[14] And the payment adjustment, as the depressing stories in newspapers have been showing, can amount to as much or more than a thousand dollars, making the homes completely unaffordable for many families.

Do not the billions in resets hitting the nation's homeowners represent debt on consumer balance sheets that most didn't even know was there?

While the Fed says about a third of total American wealth is in our homes, the percentage is substantially higher for the bottom third of the nation's wage earners. I think economists' continual focus on the nation's aggregate wealth, which is indeed quite healthy, is not giving us a clear picture of what could be happening to a large number of heavily-indebted American families that are losing their homes and have little to fall back on. Since the subprime mortgage crisis has only recently emerged, it remains to be seen how deeply emerging affluent poverty will affect the overall economy.

Chapter 12

As the Fed Cuts Rates This Time, Could the Dollar Finally Collapse?

The Reserve Act lets us print all we'll need. And it won't frighten people. It won't look like stage money. It'll be money that looks like money.
TREASURY SECRETARY WILLIAM WOODEN, 1933[1]

With the 2007 reduction in the federal funds rate, the main instrument the Federal Reserve uses to steer the economy, the Fed ended the policy of monetary tightening it began in the summer of 2004 to keep inflation from rising. At that time the fed funds rate—which is the interest rate at which banks lend to one another—was at a mere one percent, significantly lower than the inflation rate. While the consequent negative real interest rate that the Fed effectively maintained for three years gave a boost to economic growth, it also encouraged consumers to borrow, not put money in low-yielding CDs or other forms of savings, and was the primary driver of the national credit boom and our deep current account deficit.

Now that the economy is slowing down—most notably in the housing market—and inflation, though not falling much yet, could decline as a

95

result of slower economic activity, the Fed has begun injecting liquidity into the system once again. As discussed in Chapter 10, the Fed is far more worried about deflation than inflation. And though climbing oil and food prices have raised a red flag of inflationary concern, the inflation rate remains quite low by historical standards, in part because wages, which contribute to higher final prices, have remained contained. This is not the 1970s, when labor-demanded wage hikes contributed to galloping inflation. There is no labor agitation today—quite the contrary: In 2007 seventeen thousand auto workers at Delphi accepted huge pay cuts and Ford, GM, and Daimler Chrysler stocks enjoyed a strong rally mostly on expectations of labor concessions across the automobile sector. Whether due to worker concerns about losing their jobs or global outsourcing, or because unemployment is mismeasured and actually higher, as some economists argue, it is a fact that companies have been able to keep a lid on wages, which is one of the most important factors behind our low inflation rate. (See Figure 12.1).

This economic juncture during which the Fed has begun reducing short term interest rates may seem like others in the past, and many on Wall Street are preparing for further rate cuts, with all the positive economic implications

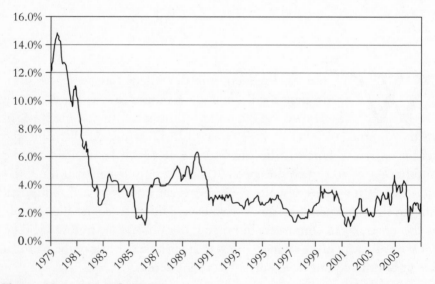

Figure 12.1   U.S. Inflation Rate
SOURCE: Bureau of Labor Statistics.

that *un*tightening usually implies, like a recovery in the real estate market. However, the crossroads the Fed has arrived at today differs substantially from all other turning points in its history because of the dollar.

The dollar's value versus other currencies and gold—a reflection of the financial world's view on our economy's growth prospects, deficits, and the attractiveness of investing in dollar-denominated instruments— has been falling, with brief interruptions, for most of this decade. Though high short-term interest rates (which usually reflect a strong economy) are generally good for the dollar, in the last year our currency has fallen below the lowest point in its post–Bretton Woods history and the reason is clear. For the first time in many years, the rest of the world is growing more rapidly than the United States, and rising interest rates in other countries are pulling investment flows out of dollars.

With interest rates that are only slightly higher than those in say, Germany, there is little compensation for investors concerned about the continuing need to fund the American current account deficit, and consequently the dollar has fallen to new record lows against the euro. The widely followed DXY index, which compares the dollar to a basket of six major currencies including the euro, broke through the critical 80 level (See Figure 12.2) that it had never convincingly violated since

Figure 12.2   Dollar vs. World's Major Currencies
SOURCE: Bloomberg.

currencies began trading freely against the dollar in the early '70s. This is a significant event for technical analysts watching currency charts, as it makes the dollar even more vulnerable to a far deeper decline.

Dormant during the 1990s, talk of a dollar crash—a sudden, sharp decline relative to other currencies that leads to inflation, spiking interest rates, and recession—has once again become common. Though statistically impossible to predict, since it has never happened, currency strategists now speak openly about the risk of a severe dollar devaluation. London's *Financial Times* and *The Economist* have been doing so for years with vehemence, and in 2005 *Newsweek* ran a cover story called "The Incredible Shrinking Dollar," which discussed the implications of a potential currency collapse.

Following Nixon's closing of the gold window and the subsequent demise of the Bretton Woods International Monetary System, economists began to ponder such a potential catastrophe, and the dollar indeed fell during the 1970s, causing inflation and economic stagnation. But no crash occurred. Warnings of doom arose once more in the 1980s, as climbing budget deficits threatened the strong American currency inadvertently created by Fed Chairman Paul Volker's inflation-taming high interest rates. But despite incidents such as the briefly shocking stock market crash of 1987, which some have attributed to currency effects, chaos was averted in a relatively orderly decline into exchange rate tranquility.

The sense that we have been here before perhaps has helped financial markets take the dollar's adjustment in stride and the world's stock exchanges continue to perform well. Although the financial imbalances that have led to our currency's downswing are far larger than in the past, analysts, traders, and fund managers know the stock market favors optimists. Even though "eventually reality catches up," as former New York Federal Reserve President Anthony Salomon warned of our large deficits, market players know the poor odds that reality faces any given year in today's financial world. Mr. Salomon's warning was made 18 years ago and yet the dollar has remained, until very recently, a virtually unquestioned store of financial value.[2]

But the economic imbalances we face today are far more significant. Our half-trillion-dollar trade deficit reached an all-time high in 2006 and the federal debt passed the nine-trillion-dollar mark, and that's excluding the tens of trillions in unfunded liabilities. The White House still deems our twin deficits, trade and federal budget, as manageable despite the market's growing concern, as reflected in the dollar's continuing slide. The "Reagan proved that deficits don't matter" argument—expressed in recent years by Vice-President Dick Cheney (former Treasury Secretary Paul O'Neill tells us)—has now been replaced by the "deficits *do* matter, and it's a good thing the dollar is showing it" rationale.[3] In this new sanguine version, the White House is allowing, even encouraging, a dollar decline so that imports fall as consumers reduce their purchases of more expensive foreign products, while our exports become more competitive abroad, a net gain for the U. S. economy.

Memories of the 1980s, when industrial companies made uncompetitive by a climbing dollar laid off a large number of blue-collar Americans—and substantial productive capacity moved to Asia—could stir up some degree of optimism about our falling dollar. Outpriced American grain farmers, who lost more than a third of their global market share in the early '80s, would undoubtedly benefit from a much weaker dollar.[4] Europeans are traveling to destinations such as Florida and New York City like never before, thanks to their improved purchasing power, a boon to our tourism industry. Boeing, selling planes in dollars, has a significant edge on Airbus, its Europe-based rival. If the dollar falls further, U.S. automakers, squeezed by rising costs and price-sensitive U.S. consumers, may gain from rising foreign currency-denominated sales abroad as its competitors sweat to become more competitive. Former Chrysler CEO Lee Iacocca, who twenty years ago complained to Washington of "Japan's $2,000 per car advantage in U.S. showrooms," would have less to say about a yen trading at 112 to the dollar versus 235 back then.[5]

While important U.S. industries stand to gain from the weaker greenback, our position as a services-based economy—where healthcare alone accounts for a hefty 17 percent of total consumer spending—is likely to make for a modest overall economic benefit. Exports represent little more than a tenth of the economy, while imports are a hefty 50 percent larger. This means that the trade deficit deteriorates every year, even if U.S. exports and imports grow at the same rate. Unfortunately, imports have been growing at a significantly faster clip recently, mainly because of higher oil prices.

As a result of this expanding trade imbalance, the United States is now consuming six percent of the GDP more than it produces, a gap funded by foreign capital. The hope is, of course, that a lower dollar will reduce the trade deficit, but the imbalance is such that the scale of devaluation would have to be very significant for it to have a palpable effect. How much? Considering the size of the deficit, some estimate that to reduce it by a mere two percentage points would require not only a further 20–25 percent decline in the dollar, but a significantly tighter budget in Washington, as well.

Such a deep currency adjustment—and some believe a deeper one is needed—would have a profound impact on many other countries, most notably the world's export economies. U.S. consumption represents close to 20 percent of global GDP. If our demand for imports began declining rapidly because of a weak dollar, Japan, Canada, Switzerland, Mexico, South Korea, Germany, Taiwan, China, Italy, and many other smaller economies would stand to lose. Buying fewer of their goods, we would provoke weaker economic growth on their part in a nascent dynamic that would certainly curtail their demand for *our* exports to some extent. Furthermore, domestic demand in Europe and Japan is notoriously sluggish already—at least by U.S. standards—as consumers in these economies save more than we and have older populations that are less prone to spend their retirement income. Their propensity to consume would be even less if lay-offs provoked by their stronger currencies began to be announced. As such, although our exports stand to benefit from a weakening dollar, one should wonder how strong the demand for our products would be should the greenback devalue further.

Another problem related with a further devaluation of the dollar lies in its inflationary implications, which could place the Fed in a catch-22 situation. Historical data, monetary history expert Barry Eichengreen warned a few years ago, shows that a 10 percent fall in the dollar produces three additional percentage points of inflation, meaning prices could rise sharply if the dollar were to decline by that much.[6] Fortunately, history has been a poor predictor in recent years as inflation remains low, a reflection, no doubt, of exporters' willingness to keep their prices for the U.S. market low to remain competitive. But that the dollar's deep fall this century has yet to cause significantly higher prices does not necessarily mean that our economy's tremendous productivity will prevent their eventual appearance.

Inflationary pressures are clearly rising, as oil and other commodity price increases creep their way into the prices of other goods and services.

But so far, other factors have kept a lid on the consumer price index, most notably our low-priced imports from China and other low labor cost economies. But this could change with a further devaluation of the dollar if Chinese exporters finally balk at their declining export prices and decide to charge more. In an interview in late 2004—the last time the dollar was almost as weak as it is now—an executive at Guandong Galanz Enterprise, the world's biggest microwave oven maker, said the company could no longer make a profit doing business with Walmart, its biggest client, partly as a result of the weak dollar.[7] As Guandong and other Chinese companies run out of ways to keep a lid on the prices they charge in a weakening currency, some economists are beginning to expect that China's next export could be inflation—after years of keeping U.S. prices low. Higher inflation would inevitably tie the hands of the Fed, which would have to raise interest rates, putting the brakes on our economy and making our debts more difficult to service. The world economy as we know it relies on a strong dollar.

That the Bush Administration has "allowed" the dollar to fall, as if it had the power to reverse the downward trend at any moment, has become a myth in currency markets. Embracing hard-for-Congress-to-swallow government spending cuts, aimed at federal debt reduction, or a tax hike (anathema to the Bush administration) would likely help the dollar recover. But in the absence of such tough medicine, the White House is almost powerless to boost the greenback through intervention—actually stepping in and buying dollars—unless the market, that amorphous collection of financial decision-makers staring at computer screens across the globe, consents to it. The foreign currency reserves we have on hand (which are needed as dollars cannot be bought with dollars) are a trifle in the vast foreign currency market where two trillion dollars are traded *daily*. To put this amount into perspective, consider that in one month currency traders exchange the equivalent of global GDP; *our* GDP changes hands almost every week. Former Treasury Secretary Robert Rubin wrote in his White House memoirs that currency trading flows are "simply too vast for such interventions to have more than a momentary effect."[8] It is striking that present foreign currency trading volume is substantially higher than what he saw in the late nineties, and more than double the level of 1992.

As such, the U.S. government can only manage the value of the dollar relative to other currencies with the cooperation of other world governments and their central banks, which can use their own currencies to prevent a dollar collapse. The success of the Plaza Accord of 1985, when leaders of the world's five largest economies cooperated to manage a decline in the dollar, provides hope for another such agreement. But the global environment today is dramatically different. Although Reagan's budget deficits were larger than Bush's in relation to the size of the U.S. economy, the dollar was strong mostly thanks to high interest rates. U.S. real (inflation-adjusted) interest rates of 7 percent on 10-year bonds provided foreign investors with an irresistible return compared with the less than one percent earned after inflation today. Though economists in the mid-1980s were growing concerned at the rising current account deficit, which had reached $100 billion for the first time, they never imagined that the deficit would balloon to *six times* that amount by 2007. Today, in contrast with 1985, the dollar's fall begins from a position of monetary weakness, not strength. World governments were then encouraging the dollar to fall; today, they tremble at the thought.

Some worry that the cohesive international environment of the 1980s, when free market economies remained united largely by a common political enemy, is absent today. In an interview in 2004, Joseph Quinlan, chief market strategist for Bank of America Capital Management, pointed out that the perception of the United States as a "rogue nation" could be a key force behind the dollar's decline. "No more guns and butter, or wads of foreign cash for a nation deeply enmeshed in the Middle East, heavily indebted at home and seemingly disengaged—some might say—from the rest of the world."[9] But this idea is beyond the reality of financial markets: capital will find its way to attractive returns, regardless of politics and morality. Communist China is the world's biggest magnet for foreign direct investment despite its appalling human rights record; the stocks of defense companies (the ones making machines and ammunition used in the killing of human beings) and producers of cancer-causing cigarettes are performing quite well these days. If you won't invest in them, someone else will. Iraq matters, but it doesn't.

The problem with the dollar is that nobody really wants it to fall this time. Asia, led by China and Japan, have been fighting desperately in recent years to maintain their currency competitiveness. How desperately? After average reserve growth of about $20 billion per month in 2006, China more than *doubled* that pace in 2007: its foreign reserves rose by one million dollars per minute during the first quarter. Although the yen has weakened slightly in recent years, in 2004 Japan intervened massively, buying mountains of dollars and U.S. securities the equivalent of three percent of U.S. GDP: its Ministry of Finance was authorized yens of monetary ammunition equivalent to *five percent* of our GDP—that means the ability to buy a stunning half trillion dollars. This is almost 30 times the $18 billion *all* of the world's five largest economies used to deflate the dollar in 1985.[10]

When China enters the currency market to buy dollars, it pays with yuan and hence injects liquidity into its economy; Russia does the same with rubles, Japan with yen, and other countries with their own domestic currencies. But to prevent the flood of liquidity from causing inflation or runaway asset bubbles, central banks try to "sterilize" their intervention by offering bonds on the market that can absorb the excess money in circulation. Unfortunately China, which lacks a well-developed domestic bond market, is unable to sop up as much liquidity as its leaders would like, and this has indirectly resulted in tremendous asset bubbles in real estate and on the stock market in recent years.

If the dollar were to come under further pressure, this would imply adding additional fuel to the inflationary flames heating up in China and the central bank might eventually be forced to reduce its dollar purchases. But for now, China remains unwilling to allow its currency to float—and let the dollar fall—because of the deep impact doing so would have on its export economy: Unemployment would simply surge. Consequently, in an effort to maintain an undervalued currency, it and Japan remain the world's two largest dollar hoarders, having accumulated well over a trillion dollars in U.S. financial assets.

The implications of this economic discussion are, in many ways, truly alarming. Over the last six years, the world's central banks have been absorbing trillions of dollars effectively to prevent the U.S. currency from collapsing. By turning around and investing these dollars in U.S. debt securities—hence lending hundreds of billions to us—they have maintained low borrowing rates that have indirectly encouraged American consumers, the world's biggest customer, to borrow our way into believing we are becoming wealthier thanks to climbing asset values, and not higher salaries. As discussed in the previous chapter, inflation-adjusted wages, particularly those of the 80 percent of Americans on the non-managerial payroll, have been stagnant for years. Meanwhile, by injecting their own economies with unprecedented amounts of liquidity—printing much of the new money used to buy the dollars investors are dumping—many central banks may have created massive asset bubbles on their own territories, thanks to the widespread, easy-to-obtain credit that banks can offer because of never-ending liquidity.

Consider the dynamic that has been unfolding in recent years: Our massive debt and deficits cause the dollar to fall, which prompts foreign central banks to buy dollars and invest in U.S. securities, which pushes down our borrowing costs, which causes our debt to rise, which causes the dollar to fall...

Before the real estate market began to sag badly in 2006, the average price of a house—the American family's most important asset—had not been climbing in line with incomes, as had traditionally been the case: It had been soaring alongside the climbing mortgage debt Americans have incurred to buy the houses, a whopping five trillion dollars. But now, record foreclosures and a rapidly climbing number of properties on the market have reminded many of us that investing in real estate is truly a risky proposition, one that involves paying a mortgage, maintenance expenses, insurance and taxes, an investment that actually sucks money out of your wallet and is not easy to sell in a hurry. And unfortunately, the portion of our incomes that Americans now use for making debt payments, most of which goes toward our mortgages, has never been higher.

In the two previous chapters, I suggested that excessive levels of consumer debt may be laying the foundation for a balance sheet recession in the United States. Though making a formal economic argument for this is beyond the scope of this book, I believe there is an emerging group of American households that are living in what I call affluent poverty—rich in possessions like houses, vehicles, and multiple consumer goods, and yet effectively poor, as so much was borrowed to finance the acquisitions that many are living in negative equity without knowing it. The average American household is cash flow negative—expenses are higher than income, and debt is the subsidy that makes ends meet, which is hardly a sign of rising wealth.

Although the Fed's frequently mentioned Flow of Funds report shows that the average American household is wealthier than ever, I think this measure is unduly influenced by the very wealthiest in the country, which pull the balance upward, and create an illusion of generalized prosperity. How else to explain the multiple signs of consumer financial distress that the country is presently witnessing? Difficult as it is to believe in such a possibility, considering the seemingly affluent times in which we live, let us think the unthinkable for a moment.

If real estate values continue to fall—as many are expecting—causing worried consumers to rein in their spending, economic growth would suffer and long before a recession, the Fed would reduce short term interest rates—that is, effectively print money to reactivate the economy. However, lower rates would prompt foreign capital to flow out of our markets and cause the dollar to fall, perhaps very sharply, which would force other central banks to buy even larger amounts of U.S. currency than the enormous quantities they have been buying already. To enter the market and buy more dollars, they would be forced to flood their own markets with even more liquidity. Consider that the money supply of Russia, another major dollar-propper, is growing at a stunning 60 percent a year!

But what if, as occurred during the last rate-cutting period that began in 2001—the one during which Ben Bernanke openly considered unconventional monetary measures—the Fed is forced to cut interest rates deeply to reactivate our debt-reliant economy? At the time those rate cuts were made, debt was 340 percent of GDP. Today, as a direct result of that widely lauded and seemingly successful monetary intervention, the addition of another $12.3 trillion in debt to American balance sheets raised that percentage to a mammoth 370 percent of our economy. So, considering our significantly larger debt, much of which was incurred at lower rates than those we see today, perhaps the Fed would have to go even lower than the one percent rate reached four years ago. This is what happened in Japan: eventually rates were slashed down to *one-fourth of a percentage point* in an effort to reactivate the economy. And the policy was unsuccessful for years because people and companies simply stopped borrowing.

Perhaps it is possible that the Fed could once again slash rates as far down as one percent, or lower. Today, this is unlikely because the dollar, whose value is now clearly out of the Fed and U.S. government's control, would likely collapse long before we even approached two percent. It is difficult to imagine China, as well as other countries, absorbing the one, two, or three *more* trillion dollars being dumped by the investment community and stand by as U.S. debt expanded to 400 percent of GDP or higher. Something would have to give under the new tidal wave of global money printing, most likely driven by unforeseen events in the colossal derivatives market, which is now half a quadrillion in size. The Long Term Capital Management blow-up in the late '90s nearly brought the financial system to a standstill. Considering that more than a third of all financial securities are denominated in dollars, the consequences of a dollar collapse are too difficult to visualize. It is sufficient to say that it would lead to a devastating global recession.

Like a capital-consuming leviathan, our trillions of dollars in annual credit-driven spending have risen over the years to absorb much of the world's savings. Our debts, rising much faster than our GDP in every year of this century, are the world's assets. Our dollars, now more than half of global central bank reserves, are claims backed by faith in Americans' ability to control spending, to maintain the value of our I-owe-all-of-yous. Over the last one hundred years, doubts about ability to pay have driven many countries—Germany, Brazil, and South Korea, to name a handful—into deep and protracted recessions due to currency devaluation, a financial disaster that our nation has fortunately been spared.

The strong possibility of a dollar collapse is the most important reason to buy gold. If this catastrophe were to unfold, I believe the value of no other financial asset would rise faster. But there are other reasons why gold should rise, as the next chapter explains.

Part Four

THE CASE FOR GOLD

Chapter 13

Why the Time Is Right for Gold to Skyrocket

Gold is often regarded as a bad investment, or even no investment at all. How else could you describe a financial asset that pays no interest, offers no earnings or dividend and whose growth is zero? The precious metal's value is derived in part from its rarity, yet it is not so uncommon as a fine work of art and is as easy to buy at a competitive price as anything offered on Amazon.com. Gold is indestructible by nature: It is non-tarnishable, cannot be corroded by any natural acid, and after lying for centuries in ocean-sunken vessels it will always be able to shine once again. Surprisingly soft as putty, even primitive gold-smiths could hammer it into wafers only a five-millionth of an inch thick. An ounce of gold can be beaten into a sheet covering nearly a hundred square feet; it is so ductile that a single ounce can be stretched into fifty miles of gold wire or plated onto copper or silver wire one thousand miles long.[1]

Though beautiful in earrings, cuff links, and dental marvels appreciated by some, one cannot project gold's earnings; and lacking a price-to-
earnings multiple, its fundamental valuation or potential take-over appeal
cannot be estimated. To the frustration of personal financial advisors and
institutional asset allocators I speak with—specialists that weight stocks,
bonds, and other assets in portfolios based on expected growth and risk—
gold cannot be modeled: There is no reliable way to forecast whether the
precious metal will rise or fall 10 percent next year. No Google-like stock
market exciter, a refined ounce of gold minted into one of the many bullion investment presentations one can find—an American Eagle, a South
African Kruggerand, or a Canadian Maple Leaf—just sits there, like a paper
weight. And its price can also just sit there, as a great many disappointed
investors have discovered over the years.

While gold surged into the hundreds of dollars per ounce beginning
in 1971 (see Figure 13.1), after then-President Richard Nixon put an end
to the decades-old gold peg at $35 an ounce, it was surely a source of
intense frustration to the many derisively called gold bugs who held onto
their precious metal during the two decades that began in 1980. Proving
once again that timing is everything in finance, that was the year when
perhaps the most spectacular opportunity to buy stocks and bonds arrived,
shortly after *BusinessWeek* announced "The Death of Equities" on its
cover. It was also the year that gold began falling from its peak of $850 dol-
lars an ounce and would decline all the way to $288 by the end of the
1990s while stocks surged (see Figure 13.2). Although the precious metal
has been recovering since then, gold is still below its peak; and if you
adjust the price for inflation, it is a striking 42 percent below its level in
1980, 27 years ago. (See Figure 13.3.)

Gold thrived during the sagging stock market of the 1970s and lan-
guished in the '80s and '90s boom in part because it is the ultimate anti-
stock: It tends not to go down, and often rises when the stock market falls, a
financial peculiarity known as negative correlation. Considering its inverse
relationship with stocks most, though not all of the time, gold is often
regarded as portfolio insurance, though it does not pay interest the way a
so-called risk-free government bond does. But gold's advantage over these
and other interest-paying investments lies in the precious metal's protection
against both inflation and a decline in the value of the dollar, risks that only
some American bonds can evade. (A strict monetarist like Milton Friedman
would argue that these risks are one and the same because "inflation is

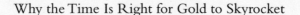

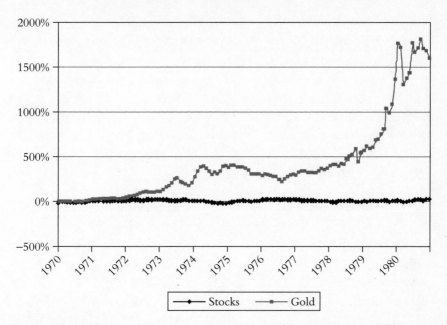

Figure 13.1   Gold Performance vs. Dow Industrial Average (1970–1980)
Source: Bloomberg.

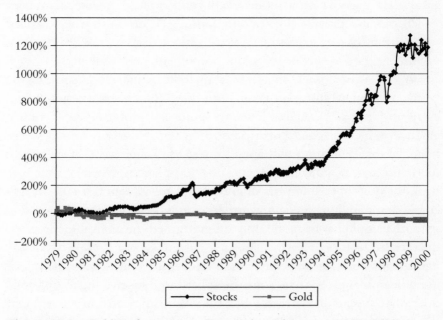

Figure 13.2   Gold Performance vs. Dow Industrial Average (1980–2000)
Source: Bloomberg.

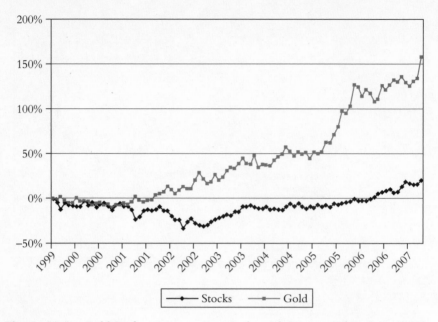

Figure 13.3 Gold Performance vs. Dow Industrial Average (2000–Sept. 2007)
SOURCE: Bloomberg.

always and everywhere a monetary phenomenon."[2]) Unlike derivatives, which can also provide financial insurance, gold does not have so-called counterparty risk—the possibility, often ignored, that the "insurer" does not pay up. Unlike so many assets, gold is not someone else's liability.

Gold's most notable investment attribute is that it remains, in the words of financial historian Peter Bernstein, "the ultimate certainty and escape from risk."[3] When all else fails, gold does not. But the fortunate absence of a protracted global catastrophe capable of provoking severe financial disruption, notwithstanding tragedies such as 9/11, is one of the main reasons gold has become the most underowned of all major financial assets in recent times, almost completely absent from the world's largest multi-billion-dollar investment funds. And yet ironically, along with silver, gold has been the only unquestioned store of value for much of recorded history. Every single paper currency—bar none—has devalued against gold and for centuries it was regarded as the foundation of the global financial system, something hard to conceive today. But consider that 93 years ago, Treasury Secretary William McAdoo ordered that the New York Stock Exchange be shut down for four long months solely to protect the nation's gold supply.[4]

Long gone are the days when gold was held, as a matter of basic financial principle, to protect wealth against potentially profligate governments printing money into worthlessness. Today, when evidence for excess supply of the world's most important currency is available for all to see—and economists speak of it openly—there is more trust than ever in the value of paper money. It is only during the last generation—that is, less than one percent of more than 6,000 years of human civilization—that gold is virtually ignored as a store of wealth.

Unpromising as gold is to most, considering the metal's 2,300 percent gain in nine years during the 1970s—one of the most spectacular runs by any financial asset class in history—evidently there have been times to profit tremendously from owning it. And time has shown that, in the absence of war or some terrible disaster that would naturally make its value rise, there are two key catalysts for gold to rally. The first is a decline in the value of paper currencies led by the dollar (with the consequent threat of rising inflation), a phenomenon that the world is experiencing at present. This is so important an occurrence that the preceding three parts of this book were tied directly to discussing the factors pointing to a deep dollar devaluation, and perhaps a collapse. These include the weakening economy led by a real estate bust and the national debt problem and negative savings rate, as reflected in our deep current account deficit.

Another important driver of investment flows into gold is the growing lack of attractive opportunities sufficient to compensate investors for the risks rising in financial markets today. As stock, bond, and other investment holders grow concerned about disappointing investment returns as the possibility of recession increases, money should begin to flow rapidly into gold, a tiny market in the ocean of liquidity that exists today. Another, relatively new driver of gold prices is the diminishing growth of new supply on the market and booming demand for gold from increasingly affluent Asian consumers, who have long been gold investors.

A dollar crash, unprecedented in the currency's history, would lead to an immediate severe disruption in global financial markets, a spike in inflation and skyrocketing interest rates that would push the economy into a sudden sharp recession that the Fed could be powerless to remedy. Considering that more than a third of the world's assets are denominated in dollars—and 60 percent of all American currency is outside our borders—the devastation that generalized panic selling of our currency would cause for the global economy cannot be measured with precision.[5]

Sudden and terrible currency crashes like the Argentinean 2001 devaluation are seldom predicted by the world's economists, despite the well-flagged crash-causing deficits accumulating for years, and yet are very common in economic history. Our present predicament reminds me of what then Deutsche Bank Mexican Economist Oscar Vera told me about the 1994 Mexican devaluation: "Economists were saying there won't be a devaluation because that would be a disaster. Well, there *was* a devaluation and it *was* a disaster." Currency crashes result, quite simply, from a country's overspending during some time followed by external creditors suddenly refusing to allow debts to continue mounting. Early signs of credit being cut off lead to frantic selling of the afflicted nation's currency and assets, a process intensified and accelerated by liquid and instantly-connected global financial markets. If deep devaluations have afflicted a great many large economies over the last century, like Germany, France, Japan, Britain, and hundreds of smaller economies, why should the United States remain the exception? Because China will continue lending to us forever? The conditions are present for a dollar crash.

Even if the dollar continues to fall gradually, our bulging national liabilities, the sudden and sharp decline in real estate values, and continuing weak spending by the debt-laden U.S. consumer are likely to lead our economy into increasingly unpredictable, and yet difficult times—under the growing influence of our external creditors. Though our country has been consuming substantially more than we produce for many years now, the credit-driven trend has not changed despite the weakening dollar, which many economists had been anticipating would reduce our (increasingly expensive) imports like oil and expand our (more attractively priced) exports. Unfortunately, as many economists have been warning for years, our industrial base has been continually decimated over the years and exports are now half the size of our booming imports. What are we going to export our way out of the trade deficit with? Asia's trade surpluses continue to soar and our trade deficit continues to worsen, as Figure 13.4 shows.

Today, the United States relies on the bulk of the world's savings to continue growing at the present pace, and to absorb them our debt to foreign investors continues to surge, as do our debt payments to them. That these savings are attracted by higher American investment returns, as is so often read in optimistic newspapers columns, has a logic that is difficult

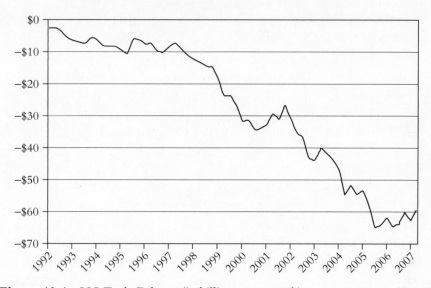

Figure 13.4   U.S. Trade Balance (in billions per month)
SOURCE: U.S. Census Bureau.

to follow. U.S. financial markets have been underperforming foreign ones for years now, a phenomenon intensified by the falling dollar. All those savings aren't going into Apple and Google shares. Investment is attracted to the United States in large part because foreign central banks are propping up the dollar to keep their companies' prices competitive in the global market. And the increasing flow of money into the world's other currencies is forcing central banks to buy more and more dollars.

The Indian rupee, to cite an example of so many rising currencies, climbed to a nine-year high against the dollar in August 2007. With a stronger currency, Indian export growth slowed to 13 percent in the first half of the year and the country's top four software exporters warned that a rising rupee had negatively affected earnings.[6] This prompted a response from monetary authorities similar to that seen among central bankers across the world: India is buying even more dollars to maintain currency competitiveness. (See Figure 13.5.) Foreign exchange reserves rose by $12 billion during July—twice as fast as they had been rising in June. The world's authorities continue to buy our collapsing dollar.

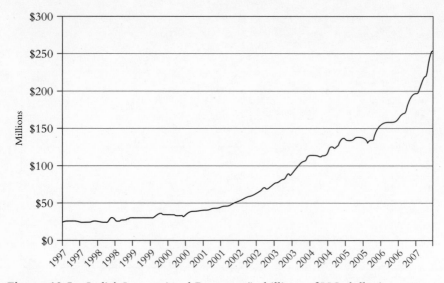

Figure 13.5   India's International Reserves (in billions of U.S. dollars)
SOURCE: Reserve Bank of India.

With debt representing a never-before experienced 370 percent of GDP—or roughly 100 percent of global GDP—our going into a severe balance sheet recession has risen as a distinct possibility. This is an economic malady that monetary authorities and the government have few weapons to fight against, as we have seen in Japan's recent experience: Japanese authorities were unable to convince companies and families to borrow more and spend when the latter were trying desperately to repair their debt-laden balance sheets. They were too busy paying down their liabilities. Unfortunately, we lack the deep savings that Japanese consumers had when recession hit that nation, which has long enjoyed a huge current account surplus. The yen did not collapse in part because it did not rely on external fund flows to support it; the dollar is entirely dependent on a steady flow of foreign investment—$2 billion per day.

The second catalyst for gold lies in an increasing lack of opportunities for profit in financial alternatives. Much like 1980 was a vital fork in the road for gold to head south and stocks and bonds to go north—way north—I think today we are approaching the reverse turning point. As I will discuss in the next chapter, following an unprecedented historical run, stocks, bonds, and many other financial assets face formidable obstacles—particularly because our consumer-driven economy is weakening, corporate profit margins are at 50-year highs, and monetary and fiscal stimuli have been used so aggressively in recent years. Bond yields are at unappealing multi-decade lows and stocks are trading at attractive multiples only if you expect the present off-the-charts profit boom to persist. Additionally, a great many alternative opportunities—like real estate investment and private equity—have boomed like never before, making their continued strong performance increasingly improbable, especially considering the large number of players competing for increasingly slim margins. And their source of cheap financing has been drying up lately, provoking last summer's financial turmoil.

Meanwhile, in addition to overstretched financial markets and the dollar risk, investors have ridden the waves of easy credit to their advantage using leveraged investment strategies to enhance their returns, a factor that has led to many chapters of financial instability in the past—most notably in the fall of 1929. Margin debt levels on the New York Stock Exchange are once again at pre-2000 market crash levels.[7] "What is unusual about this equity market cycle," says Morgan Stanley economist Gerard Minack, is that debt was first built up amongst investors, followed by companies levering up to buy back shares of one another in recent years. "Ultimately, we could end up with triple-layered leverage: leveraged investors owning leveraged companies that depend on leveraged consumers."[8]

While risks like a potential dollar crash and a lack of attractive investment opportunities can push gold up, a third worrisome concern was almost completely absent during the 1970s gold boom—derivatives, financial instruments that pose the least understood and most difficult to measure systemic threat to the global financial system. Growing from a miniscule market 30 years ago, the notional value of derivatives contracts (the dollar amount upon which contracts are based) has ballooned to $415 trillion, an unfathomable amount more than six times larger than global GDP.[9] This quantity is striking when compared with the less than $70 trillion that existed when the fund Long Term Capital Management—which at one point had a total derivative book of $1.25 trillion and was leveraged at 100 times its underlying equity—nearly brought the global financial system to its knees a decade ago.[10] The credit derivatives market alone now exceeds $30 trillion in value, seven times the level of just four years ago. Today the $13 trillion in derivatives based on corporate bonds are more than twice the size of the bond market itself.

Turning pages of the dense 2005 Report of the Counterparty Risk Management Policy Group II, the second report published following the LTCM meltdown to evaluate global financial market risks related with derivatives, a reader is faced repeatedly with the word "complexity". Aiming to reassure financial market participants, the lengthy report, signed by former New York Fed President Gerald Corrigan and 13 other financial heavy-hitters, reads more like an encyclopedia of all that can go wrong in financial markets today. In it, one reads of the difficulty in measuring financial risk in highly complex credit transactions against the total risk in a credit instrument portfolio;[11] how unknown consequences can result from leveraged investors in a crowded trade that are compelled to try and liquidate or immunize positions at the same time;[12] and why, though an LTCM disaster is unlikely today, a new crash could be a highly correlated event involving multiple hedge funds—the number of which has more than doubled since LTCM—and whose intensity cannot be forecasted.[13]

The world's economic authorities are growing increasingly concerned, especially now that market volatility, which has a direct impact on the derivatives market, has doubled since early 2007. Speaking that year about complex contracts such as credit default swaps and swaptions, European Central Bank President Jean-Claude Trichet said, "There is now such creativity of new and very sophisticated financial instruments . . . that we don't know fully where the risks are located." He added: "We are trying to understand what is going on but it is a big, big challenge."[14] The International Monetary Fund's Global Financial Stability Report has pointed out that risk management systems designed to deal with new complex products have yet to face a live test.[15] It is worth remembering that the first important test for derivatives, the LTCM blow-up, was a blatant disaster left unresolved in the market: The Fed forced a group of the world's biggest banks to lend the disgraced fund out of its troubles. LTCM showed the world that derivatives, which were created as a cost-effective method of controlling financial risk, have become an entirely new and massive asset class, which the financial gamblers of the world can speculate on regardless of the risks this creates for the financial system.

The most worrisome aspect about the derivatives market is that most of the trillions of dollars in contracts, like the many types of interest rate and foreign currency derivatives, do not trade on a market. And since an over-the-counter derivative cannot be bought and sold like a share of IBM, it is hard to establish its price, what a buyer today would actually be willing to pay for it. The financial institutions that own non-traded derivatives have broad discretion in attaching a value to them and rarely reveal many details of their trades, which are often conducted with the handful of so-called "LCFIs", large complex financial institutions like Bank of America, J.P. Morgan Chase & Co., and UBS, which increasingly dominate the derivatives world.[16] Hence, banks, pension funds, insurance companies, hedge funds, and the many other financial institutions that own derivatives may have some assets that are worth more or perhaps a lot less than what is reported each quarter. And it is certainly in the interest of hedge fund managers, in particular, whose pay is generally closely related with performance, to price their assets with the highest possible value.[17]

The uncertain value of non-traded derivatives and the multiplicity of asset-based securities was brought to the fore very suddenly in mid-2007, when two small, yet highly leveraged Bear Stearns funds that had made failed bets on securities backed by subprime mortgages collapsed. The High-Grade Structured Credit Strategies Fund and the High-Grade Structured Credit Strategies Enhanced Leverage Fund had invested in collateralized debt obligations, credit instruments layered with assets of varying risk that are essentially derivatives, as Bill Gross of Pimco, the world's largest bond fund, has pointed out.[18] The value of the two funds, which had risen to as high as $20 billion, collapsed to virtually nothing.[19] Though small in a market where some institutions have hundreds of billions under management, the funds raised financial eyebrows across the world out of concern that a great many other illiquid securities could be similarly mispriced. If the funds had been forced by their creditors to sell their holdings in a hurry, and thereby price the securities at a low value, holders managing other funds could have been forced to "mark to market" their positions and thereby suddenly take heavy losses. This possibility likely contributed to a sharp decline in the dollar in the weeks following the Bear Stearns news, as the broad dollar index nearly broke through the 80 support level it has held above since currencies began floating freely in the early 1970s. The drop below 80 would come in the fall.

And herein lay a serious financial challenge for the new century: The dollar's vulnerability could restrict the Fed's ability to head off the next financial crisis. Most financial market participants are comforted by the thought that the Fed will always rescue financial markets in situations of illiquidity—an inability to sell assets at prices that are not distorted by the temporary market imbalances that arise from time to time. The Fed has stepped into the market at vital points in the last twenty years by injecting liquidity—that is, lending money to banks or even securities firms that can buy the assets being sold at bargain prices.

Such was the case after the stock market fell 22 percent on a single day, October 19, 1987, the steepest daily decline in financial markets history. Notwithstanding the moral hazard implied in the government propping up the stock market, Board members for the first time considered "an off-the-wall suggestion: targeted Fed lending specifically designed to support stock values," as the then highly confidential Summary Papers on Risks in the U.S. Financial System revealed.[20] This ultimate weapon was apparently not resorted to, and the Fed was able to use normal channels to provide the liquidity the market needed to rapidly bounce back from what could have been a catastrophe. But the episode and others that followed have made this much clear: The Fed will do whatever is necessary to defend financial markets from chaos.

Comforting as it to know the Fed always stands ready as a financial system guardian to provide unlimited liquidity to prevent disasters, the central bank up until recent years has been able to carry out this function without much concern about the dollar. During the late 1980s, despite climbing deficits, the dollar was rock solid thanks to attractive interest rates; and in the 1990s, a falling federal deficit, the booming economy and stock market kept the dollar firm. When the LTCM disaster erupted ten years ago, the Fed moved decisively to turn on the liquidity faucet without concern about our currency. But since the Fed began cutting interest rates in 2001, the dollar has been sinking due to our surging current account deficit, low interest rates, and the continuing underperformance of our financial markets. In fact, during the two years ending in March 2007, American institutional investors pulled a net $135 billion out of U.S. equities, implying that threats to the dollar now come from within the United States, as well.[21] In early 2007, each hint that the Fed was about to cut interest rates was met with a sharp dollar sell-off in the markets. Higher returns in other currencies, particularly in those of nations that don't have large deficits that need funding, make the dollar "vulnerable" to a drop in investment flows, as the Bank of International Settlements warned in mid-2007.[22]

Should the market turbulence that began at that time continue and more hedge fund or derivatives-linked disturbances arise, it is unlikely that the Fed will be able to act as decisively as in the Greenspan years to help financial markets stabilize. Unfortunately, concern about a sagging dollar—a decline that would likely accelerate if the Fed cut rates aggressively at this point—could make the new liquidity created actually exit the U.S. financial system, a problem that could provoke a severe downward spiral in the greenback. The dollar risk is a serious consideration in the financial markets' ever-growing need for liquidity, the lifeblood of derivatives, as financial risk management expert Richard Bookstaber explains in *A Demon of Our Own Design*.[23] "Without liquidity, derivatives markets die."[24] And if the Fed cannot provide liquidity without provoking a dollar problem, then the already gigantic derivatives risk is much deeper than believed.

Another significant risk facing the global financial system lies in China, increasingly the United States' biggest lender, whose economy is beginning to show signs of overheating under the rising levels of liquidity being created partly as a result of lending to us. To keep the dollar strong, and the yuan weak, the Chinese central bank is forced to inject large amounts of new money into its economy, and it has been unable to properly sterilize these inflows (reduce the level of domestic liquidity) with higher interest rates or reserve requirements for banks. The multiple interest rate hikes and other efforts to reduce liquidity that the country's central bank has implemented have done little to contain booming double-digit growth and rising inflation. The broad money supply was growing at 17 percent in June 2007 and Chinese authorities have been unable to contain accelerating loan growth with lending still expanding at an astonishing 19 percent annualized rate.[25] Meanwhile, the hundreds of billions in reserves Chinese authorities are forced to accumulate to keep the yuan from soaring—still mostly in dollars—are often reinvested into U.S. securities, which has helped maintain low U.S. interest rates.

There is growing speculation that the tremendous flood of money into China (and out of the dumped dollars that the Chinese central bank must buy) could eventually force it to stop buying U.S. currency to maintain a weak yuan—to secede as the 51st state of the monetary union called the United States, as Pimco's Paul McCulley said, not so amusingly.[26]

He was referring to the fact that China, having the yuan pegged to the dollar, has its monetary policy effectively governed by the Fed. Knowing that the Chinese currency is undervalued, hundreds of billions of investment dollars are being converted confidently into yuan each year, and any hint that the country's authorities might allow the currency to appreciate only intensifies the massive inflows. And speculation increases each time there is news of anti-China protectionist legislation moving through the U.S. Congress, which could force the Asian nation to let the dollar fall more rapidly. Foreign reserves exceeding well over one trillion dollars are rapidly approaching the country's entire annual GDP, and increased by a massive $266 billion during the first half of 2007 alone, an amount larger than what was accumulated in all of 2006. Liquidity creation is accelerating.

While the waves of liquidity have led to booming economic growth exceeding an amazing 11 percent per year, the unattractive negative real interest rates that Chinese banks offer have encouraged substantial money to flow away from savings and into real estate and the stock market, which doubled in value in less than a year. In early 2007, between 200,000 and 300,000 brokerage accounts were being opened every day to feed the voracious need to invest (and speculate) amongst the savings-rich Chinese population, much of which is buying stocks for the first time.[27] But skyrocketing demand is also feeding into the prices of basic goods and rising wages which may eventually provoke an inflationary wave exportable to the United States. As of the writing of this chapter, China had exported inflation to the United States for two consecutive months, according to Credit Suisse.[28] Though not his formal estimate, Credit Suisse's Dong Tao believes inflation could rise as high as eight percent in mid-2008 from under four percent in mid-2007 due to intensifying demand pressure.

For years, the continuing low prices on the wide array of products imported from China has helped offset the effect of surging oil and commodities prices on American inflation. Prices of clothing and fabric imported from China, for instance, have fallen roughly 25 percent in the United States since 1995.[29] But now Chinese producers, pressured from below by rising input and labor costs—as well as a possible surge in new environmental protection-related costs—are likely to begin demanding higher prices for the goods sold in the United States, particularly because the dollar is so weak. Prices in the United States "are artificially low," says former Morgan Stanley Asian Chief Economic Andy Xie. "You're not paying the costs of pollution, and that is why China is an environmental catastrophe."[30]

Investment risks are always present in financial markets, which must climb a wall of continual worry. But financial theory ultimately teaches that a rational investor will not invest if there is insufficient compensation for the risk involved in writing a check. What compensation is there today for barely attractive stock and bond valuations in a weakening, debt-laden U.S. economy whose currency likely has nowhere to go but down? Moving assets away from the U.S. and into foreign stock markets, as American investors have been doing in droves in recent years, has served to accelerate the dollar's decline. Meanwhile, risks of Chinese turmoil or a sudden, destabilizing disaster in the larger-than-ever derivatives market are emerging as distinct potential sources of instability that could drive financial markets down and gold higher.

Six trillion dollars in investment flows travel around the globe each year, the bulk of which are seeking the highest possible investment return at an acceptable level of risk. If returns in various asset classes begin to disappoint, gold should rise by default, as it did in the 1970s. But the striking difference with that decade is that today the amount of investment that could rush into gold is substantially larger than it was three decades ago. The total value of global assets now exceeds $140 trillion and more than a third is invested in U.S. dollars. Fifty-one trillion dollars is invested in American stocks and bonds alone.[31] If in fact there is a serious problem with the dollar—as well as with all the paper currencies being printed en masse to save the greenback—and stocks and bonds have little to offer, a trickle of liquidity into the miniscule $3 trillion gold market could make gold and other precious metals spark the next '90s Nasdaq.

At that time, as Bookstaber reminds us, Internet stocks skyrocketed largely due to a lack of float, shares in circulation, and the surging demand for scarce stock led to a phenomenal stock market boom.[32] The same could easily happen with gold, much of which has been locked in central bank and private vaults for decades. The gold the United States holds at Fort Knox, the largest gold depository in the world, has remained virtually untouched since the early 1980s (although the government did dump some gold on the market during the 1987 stock market crash).

Only three percent of all the aboveground refined gold is traded in an entire year, a mere $110 billion—which is less than what is traded in Microsoft shares in a single day. Gold has a float (the freely available amount that can be bought and sold each year) of perhaps 10,000 tons worth $220 billion, which is a fraction of the amount traded on the New York Stock Exchange in one day.

And contrary to the Nasdaq boom, which gave rise to hundreds of IPOs and hence to a growing supply of new shares for sale, the existing amount of gold cannot be expanded beyond what mining companies produce each year, merely a 1.6 percent annual increase in the amount of gold available. Supply is also being constrained by central banks that, perhaps out of concern about the rapidly weakening dollar, have reduced gold sales dramatically in the last two years and some are now buying. I think it is only a matter of time before more and more hedge funds realize that central banks can't dump gold forever to stabilize its price and perpetuate the illusion that monetary authorities have global liquidity under control. Gold cannot be printed, and it is now only nine percent of total global reserves following decades of selling by the world's central banks—and the sharp increase in dollar reserves.

Investing in gold requires a temporary change in mindset for the optimists that run the world and others that tend to feel intense disdain for precious metals. I don't play a part in running the world, but I am certainly an optimist. Working as a financial analyst in Mexico City during the 1990s, I covered two stocks, Grupo México and Sanluis, which had extensive mining operations. Talking about metals for hours, writing about them, and walking deep into mines in remote areas of Mexico, the thought of owning gold did not occur to me once. I was buying stocks like everybody else. But since 2003, when the harmful effects of negative real interest rates became apparent in a sinking dollar, a rapid decline in the national savings rate, and skyrocketing debt, I have been increasing my investments in precious metals and learning all that I can about them. Now that the real estate market is weakening sharply and a great many American consumers are so heavily indebted that they can't step in and buy a house, we are beginning to pay the price for the Fed's fixation on maintaining economic growth at the expense of increasing financial risks. American total debt (excluding the government's unfunded liabilities) was $34 trillion five years ago. Today it has reached $51 trillion.

Where the road leads now that we have become dependent on foreign creditors to maintain our consumption level is unclear, but financial risks are escalating and there is need for financial cover.

I see gold as a place to park, a tactical investment opportunity that could work for several years, but I will always keep the exit door in sight. Though enthusiasts point to its protection against the declining value of paper currencies, gold, as famed market strategist Barton Biggs has pointed out, is a "sterile investment" that "has not *enhanced* the purchasing power of its owners over the millennia."[33] Stocks have outperformed gold ten to one as the investment of choice for the long run, as the great many millionaires and billionaires like Biggs can attest to. But I think today there is a singular opportunity for gold to begin another spectacular run, while stocks and bonds rest for some time—or perhaps fall sharply—below the peak that I believe they have reached. Placing a growing lack of attractive investment opportunities into an environment of a languishing U.S. real estate market, our massive debt, a struggling dollar, China's new export of inflation, the ever-present chance of a derivatives blow-up, and perhaps a suddenly powerless Fed, I can't visualize a better time in the peacetime history of modern investment to buy gold. And so few investors own it today.

Chapter 14

Stocks and Bonds Offer Little Compensation for Risk Today

The third leg of the longest, deepest economic expansion in United States history is beginning to show its age. We have been living in truly exceptional times. While there were a few interruptions, like the recession at the turn of the '90s decade and a short one in 2001, these were mere pauses in the 25-year boom that began in 1982, and both were mild in comparison with some of the brutal recessions preceding them. The one inflation-slaying Paul Volker provoked indirectly caused a surge in bankruptcies and unemployment so severe that by 1981 he was assigned a permanent bodyguard, this after a distraught man armed with multiple weapons including a sawed-off shotgun stormed the Fed searching for its chairman.[1] But looking back from that recession, which ended in 1982, the boom has made the economy three times larger. Unemployment remains below five percent compared with close to 10 percent then. The Dow Jones Industrial Average, which was then just crossing the 1,000 mark, touched 14,000 in 2007, a remarkable gain. Though concern about rising inflation in recent months has rattled financial markets, the less than three percent rate reported over the last year remains extremely low by historical standards.

A continuing low inflation rate has been the primary support for keeping interest rates down and bond prices high. (Bond prices and interest rates have an inverse relationship: As interest rates fall, bond prices go up.) The yield on the 10-year U.S. Treasury bond, the benchmark against which most other bonds of similar maturity are compared, continues to hover around a low four percent compared with the 14 percent it was trading at in 1982 (See Figure 14.1.)

The secular decline in Treasury rates from that peak has also helped corporate, mortgage, asset-backed and other fixed income instruments— whose yields closely follow Treasury rates—enjoy falling yields over the years, as well, a boon to investors who have benefited from the consequent rise in bond prices. The attractive "spread" over Treasury instruments these bonds can offer—which compensate for additional risks that range from missed payments to corporate bankruptcy—has fallen very

Figure 14.1   Ten-Year U.S. Treasury Bond Yield
SOURCE: Bloomberg.

sharply in recent years as investors, increasingly from other countries, have pushed up their prices. Foreign central banks, attempting to recycle the trillions of dollars in reserves amassed to suppress the value of their local currencies, have been a key driver of this rush for yield, raising demand for the wide array of credit instruments to be found in U.S. markets.

While falling rates and spreads have been a boon to the economy, as companies and individuals have been able to borrow at lower interest rates, many observers warn that rates have fallen too low. By early 2007, lower credit quality bonds—the ones whose payments come from the riskiest borrowers (like subprime mortgage borrowers that are forfeiting in record numbers)—were offering the lowest premium, or reward for risk, in financial history. Over the past 20 years, the additional yield of so-called high-yield bonds over Treasuries has averaged over 5 percentage points, and have spiked to well over 10 percentage points in times of credit market stress. But in June 2007 the spread hit a record low of 2.63 percentage points, which, if the 10-year treasury rate were at 5 percent, would imply a yield of merely 7.63 percent on the riskiest of bonds. Steven Rattner, the managing principal of Quadrangle group, wrote at that time in the *Wall Street Journal* that money is available today in quantities, at prices and on terms "never seen in the 100-plus years since U.S. financial markets reached full flower."[2] The current inflated prices (and consequent low yields) in the high yield bond market, he believes, "will eventually earn quite an imposing tombstone in the graveyard of other great past manias."

During a June speech before the CFA Society of Chicago, First Pacific Advisors CEO Robert Rodriguez pointed out that the Government of Pakistan, a country with a short history of political and economic instability—it was only founded 60 years ago—last summer placed a ten-year bond yielding 6.88 percent, barely 2 percentage points above the U.S. Treasury bond yield.[3] Rodriguez's answer to the fundamental financial question, "Am I being sufficiently compensated for these apparent risks?" was clearly no. This is the important point about today's financial markets. Whether or not the price of riskier instruments in the global credit market are about to fall sharply—a forecast that, by the way, has been made repeatedly in recent years—is always difficult to predict. But absent an incentive to buy high-yield or investment grade bonds, their continued price appreciation becomes increasingly improbable, while the risk of their decline increases.

The same could be said about the stock market. Both the Dow Jones Industrial Average and the S&P 500 have clawed their way back from the collapse that began in 2000 and have climbed to new records. This rise came on the back of higher-quality and more credible profits than those being reported near the peak of the '90s boom, when several high-profile companies were later found to have been padding their earnings. The S&P 500 Index is currently trading on a price-to-earnings multiple of 16, which appears reasonable considering this is near the average P/E of the market since the end of World War II. However this multiple would not be all that attractive if we subtracted the anomalous 1990s stock market years, when the P/E shot up past 40.[4] Because, if these years are pulled out of the average, today's market valuation is not very cheap by historical standards, even though interest rates remain extremely low, which makes stocks increasingly attractive compared with bonds.

But there is something more important to point out about the present stock market's valuation: Companies have rarely had it better. Despite challenges such as a surge in commodity costs and weak pricing power, companies have successfully expanded net earnings by boosting their profit margins far higher than was thought possible. The stock market has remained strong despite the struggling real estate market and sluggish consumer spending, largely because U.S. companies have been able to keep margins at the highest in 54 years. Perhaps more strikingly, earnings per share are 74 percent above their long term trend.[5] Considering that the stock market ultimately rises on the back of rising corporate profits, margins and profits would have to remain at their present off-the-charts levels for stocks to maintain their present pace, which would be a statistical anomaly. (See Figure 14.2.)

If we followed the stock market valuation steps prescribed in Benjamin Graham and David Dodd's classic *Security Analysis*, as *New York Times* investment writer David Leonhardt reminds us, stocks would be trading at an expensive 27 times earnings—69 percent overvalued versus the average of the last 60 years.[6] This is because stocks are trading based on recent breathtaking and likely unsustainable high earnings, and not on those of a normalized seven to ten-year average as Graham and Dodd suggested in their classic text, widely regarded as the bible of value investing, a theory put in practice by men such as Warren Buffett.

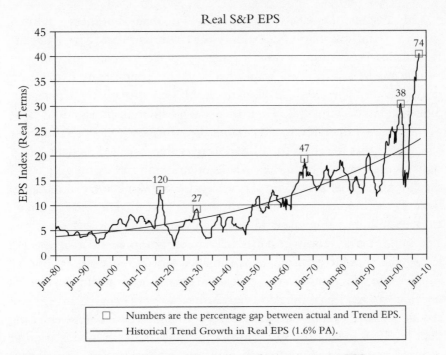

Figure 14.2   Chart of Historical Trend Growth in Corporate EPS
Sources: Standard & Poors, Robert Shiller, Bureau of Labor Statistics, Morgan Stanley.

But investors are not crazy: Stocks are trading higher because earnings have continued rising. The key to today's high market multiple (based on earnings normalized as Graham and Dodd would have prescribed) is what is commonly called visibility: The market will trade at high multiples of future earnings so long as investors remain comfortable that the numbers analysts project can be met. Stock valuations can be justified if profit margins remain at a half-century peak, if half a trillion dollars in share buy backs continue each year, and if trillions of dollars in M&A activity endure, which seems extremely unlikely. Other developed markets like Europe have similar multiples, and these are not far above those of many emerging market stocks, which used to trade at a deep discount because of the economic and political risks one assumed in owning them. It is no wonder that Wall Street analysts have turned more bearish than ever: in February 2007 buy recommendations slipped below holds as a percentage of total stock picks for the first time.[7]

Meanwhile, the first wave of 76 million baby boomers—about a quarter of the country's population—is beginning to retire in 2008, and it is unclear what impact their liquidation of stock portfolios will have on the markets in the years ahead. The aging population "is the most critical issue facing the developed world," stock-market guru Jeremy Siegel said in March 2007. Their financial portfolio disposals could cause as much as a 40 percent to 50 percent drop in asset prices, he said.[8] The age cohort that followed the baby boomers, the so-called Generation X, only number 66 million and have a negative saving rate that is even lower than the already negative national rate. Siegel, and a number of his colleagues, believes that boomers retiring in the next few years will find it difficult to find enough young savers to buy their assets.[9]

Some market commentators have been pointing out that the last leg of the present earnings expansion has not come from traditional sources, like sales growth or market share gains, but from "financial engineering," driven by credit. Although American corporate balance sheets remain healthy overall, in recent years companies have been increasing debt levels and using the proceeds to buy back shares, which is another way of increasing earnings per share. An example was IBM's announcement in April 2007 that it was boosting its dividend and buying back up to 10 percent of its shares outstanding after borrowing funds in the present low interest rate environment. The share jumped four percent that day. Johnson & Johnson enjoyed the same market reaction when it announced that it would also raise debt to buy back a whopping $10 billion of its own shares.[10] Take shares off the market—like the staggering $548 billion in shares retired in 2006—and those remaining gain scarcity value and go up in price.[11] Although levering up corporate balance sheets has provided a boost to many a share price in recent years, many remain skeptical about its potential to keep driving stock values higher. When he hears the term "financial engineering," market sage and billionaire Wilber Ross says this indicates another person "has found a way to underprice risk."[12]

Another driver of share prices has been the surge in mergers and acquisitions, the volume of which topped one trillion dollars during the first three months of 2007.[13] As if that were not amazing enough, M&A volume rose to $131 billion on a single day, April 23, 2007. But that may have been the peak. By July, the five-year run of leveraged buyouts pouring hundreds of billions into struggling industries like automobiles and newspapers appeared to be grinding to a halt. With investors finally scared away by rock-bottom rates that offered little compensation for risk, banks were forced to delay the sale of $12 billion in bonds related with the sale of Chrysler to Cerberus Capital Management. This meant that debt recycling machines J.P. Morgan Chase, Citigroup, and Goldman Sachs, among others, were forced to pony up much of the money themselves.[14] The same is true of the eight banks that attempted to sell $18.4 billion in loans for UK retailer Boots, the biggest buyout in Britain's history.[15] These roadblocks tie up dealmaker capital and may force the delay or outright cancellation of the additional $300 billion in high-yield bonds and loans, much of which is needed to fund further LBO activity, that U.S. bankers were hoping to sell for the rest of 2007.[16] For the time being, perhaps the deals that have been such a strong stock market driver will still be possible, but at higher rates that may make more and more transactions fall through.

On the sanguine view that there is always a rising market somewhere on the planet, the flow of funds into Asia, Europe, and emerging markets continues unabated. The dollar and U.S. markets could crash, the argument goes, but several other markets (not including Japan, which is underperforming like the U.S.) will continue to rise as money will need to flow somewhere. The increasingly popular notion that global growth will remain healthy as Europe and Asia decouple from the United States despite the latter's slowdown does not hold up to close scrutiny, as Lacy Hunt, an economist at Hoisington Investment Management in Austin, Texas explained in early 2007.[17]

The world is presently a mix of rapidly growing economies—like the "BRIC" countries (Brazil, Russia, India, and China)—and significantly underperforming ones, such as the United States and Japan. The United States still accounts for almost a third of the world's GDP (31 percent) and Japan 14 percent for a combined 45 percent of global growth. If one were to add the contributions of Canada (2 percent) and Mexico (2 percent), whose growth is invariably dragged down by U.S. slowdowns, we arrive at 49 percent of global economic output weakening. But even this analysis "is not a complete description" of the impact of the United States on the global economy, Hunt believes. The large and growing trade surpluses that China, India, Brazil, and Europe maintain with the United States (which play a major role in their economic growth) would clearly suffer under a slowdown in the world's largest economy. This is perhaps why most global stock markets continue to move in sync, some rising or falling faster than others, but all generally moving, historically, in the same direction. It would be an anomaly for U.S. stocks to begin weakening and for other global markets to rise.

Rising concerns don't necessarily mean one should become bearish on stocks and that their decline is imminent. In fact, there are—as always—significant reasons why the stock market could power ahead further, such as the growing number of sovereign funds putting money into equities. This is no small matter, as such funds control an estimated $2.5 *trillion* in assets. China alone is beginning to put $200 billion to work, and another $100 billion will follow soon after. In July, China and Singapore agreed to invest as much as $18.5 billion in Barclays, one of Europe's largest banks. South Korea's $223 billion National Pension Service announced plans to increase equity investments. Russia and Australia should be joining them soon.[18] Of course, there is always the possibility, should the stock market begin to sag, that these funds won't allocate substantial funds to the stock market, and that perhaps they will put a fraction into gold. The point made in this chapter is only that significant obstacles to the stock and bond markets' continuing ascent are increasing and rewards for these climbing risks are diminishing, as a growing number of market skeptics are pointing out.

Barton Biggs, a veteran of over 40 years of investing, has begun to warn of the similarities between today and the market crash of 1987, which came after a similar period of strong stock market performance.[19] In his June speech First Pacific Advisors' Rodriguez, a veteran financial expert whose FPA New Income Fund has not had a down year in 30 years, discussed the "bubble of massive proportions" he sees in the housing market and suggested house prices could fall by more than 20 percent; he delved into the multiple risks lurking in the multi-faceted credit market; he worried about the rising levels of debt among private equity players, believed to be "pushing the boundaries of prudence", and the risks being assumed by hedge funds via derivatives; and he lamented that stock market investors were directing their cash flows to the riskiest areas of the equity universe. After hearing of his deep concerns for virtually all financial markets, listeners were probably not surprised to learn that he was comfortable holding 40 percent of funds in cash, which is about as bearish as a money manager can get. Rodriguez's bet has no doubt made him suffer during the first half of 2007, as stock markets rose substantially across the world. "We are willing to bet our firm and our reputation to be right," Rodriguez said.

The rise in market risk and increasing absence of reward in the form of low prices is reminiscent of the year 1968. The stock market had enjoyed several years of strong performance, and even though there was growing concern about the falling value of the dollar, optimism was ubiquitous. There were plenty of bulls still buying in 1969, but there was a rising investment star who was quietly liquidating his firm's portfolio. Calling it quits, he actually cashed in virtually all of it after a phenomenal return exceeding 1,100 percent in the previous ten years—five times better than the Dow. This was Warren Buffett.[20] And by May of 1970, a portfolio containing every share on the Dow Industrials had lost half its value from the start of 1969.[21] The Dow experienced extensive volatility, but did not climb out of a trading range for the next decade while gold skyrocketed.

Chapter 15

Gold's Scarcity: New Sources of Demand and Falling Supply

Because the gold market is so small, a very small segment of people are capable of driving up gold prices.

ALAN GREENSPAN IN INTERVIEW WITH SHERRY COOPER,
CHIEF ECONOMIST OF BMO NESBITT BURNS, OCTOBER 6, 2006

Let me put Mr. Greenspan's observation into perspective. If, out of concern about the falling dollar and growing financial risks, investors pulled just one percent out of their investments in U.S. stocks and bonds and put the cash into gold, the precious metal's price would likely double and perhaps triple. This single percent of our core financial markets, worth roughly $440 billion, is the equivalent value of 13 percent of all the gold accumulated throughout human history, the estimated 158,000 tons owned throughout the world, less than four percent of which changes hands each year. That one percent slice of American stock and bond holdings is almost four times the value of all the gold stored by the U.S. government at Fort Knox, the biggest gold depository on the planet.* Four-hundred and forty billion dollars is equivalent to eight times what the entire global gold mining industry produces in one year, and if investors decided to move this relatively small amount out of stocks and bonds into gold, the consequent scarcity would likely provoke financial market ripples leading to a massive gold rush, as occurred in the depressing 1970s, when few other investments offered attractive returns.[1]

But even in the absence of such a dramatic event, supplies of gold are stagnating while demand continues to climb, led by new investment vehicles and booming Asian demand. (See Figure 15.1.) Over the last five years, 61 percent of the gold sold yearly in the global market has come from mine production, 14 percent from central bank sales and the recycled gold that is melted down, re-refined and reused each year accounted for the remaining

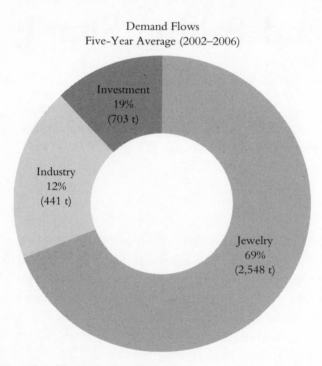

Figure 15.1   Global Demand for Gold
SOURCE: World Gold Council.

---

*Or so we are told. To the fascination of gold conspiracy theorists, no visitors have been allowed at Fort Knox since 1974 to confirm the gold is actually there.

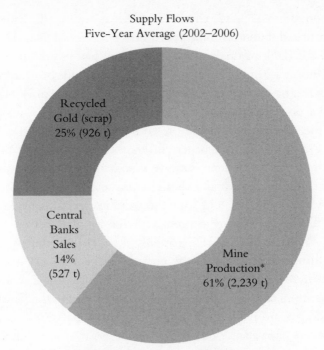

Supply Flows
Five-Year Average (2002–2006)

Recycled
Gold (scrap)
25% (926 t)

Central
Banks
Sales
14%
(527 t)

Mine
Production*
61% (2,239 t)

*Mine Production net of hedging

Figure 15.2   Global Supply Flow for Gold
SOURCE: World Gold Council.

25 percent. (See Figure 15.2.) Higher gold prices caused scrap suppliers to dump a record 1,108 tons on the market in 2006, representing a record 28 percent of supply. But even this jump in supply could not keep gold from staying above $600 an ounce throughout the year, and the average price rose 36 percent over that of 2005 driven mostly by rising investment demand. Of the three sources of supply, central banks and the mining industry have been reducing the amount of gold sold into the market for several reasons that are worth discussing in detail.

Central banks, like the Bank of England and the Bank of France, have long been dumping their large gold supplies onto the market for reasons rarely elucidated by monetary authorities. One reason could be that gold is a less liquid asset (at least for an owner of tons) than currency reserves, and perhaps central banks have thought it has made sense to convert gold into paper currency when prices climb. However, central banks have shown a willingness to sell gold even when prices drop to record lows. This was the case when the Bank of England sold more than half its gold reserves—400 tons—in 1999 at a 20-year low price. The decision, made by Gordon Brown, has returned to haunt him now that he is prime minister of Britain.[2]

Another possible reason is that some monetary decision-makers wonder what the use of holding the precious metal is when most believe it would be impossible to have paper currencies backed by gold again. At its inception in 1913, the Federal Reserve was required to hold gold reserves equivalent to 40 percent of all bills and coins in circulation.[3] The dollar at one time was really worth gold, something our leaders took pride in. But to return to this gold standard at present prices, even if the Fed were able to buy *all of the gold in the world*—roughly three trillion dollars worth—it still would not own enough of the precious metal to back 40 percent of the more than $10 trillion in the United States' broad monetary base[4]: in the wake of the monetary explosion we have experienced in the last three decades, our dollars are really so abundant and gold that scarce. But even if central bankers have abandoned the possibility of ever returning to a gold standard, as monetary authorities they no doubt remain well aware of the continuing importance of gold, as Alan Greenspan made clear in 1999: "Gold still represents the ultimate form of payment in the world. . . . Fiat money paper in extremis is accepted by nobody. Gold is always accepted."[5]

A final and perhaps more realistic reason why central banks may have been dumping gold is that doing so, which pushes down the price of the precious metal, gives the impression that financial risks and inflation, in particular, are under control. Keeping firm control over the national price level is the most important goal of any central bank. When the price of gold rises, as it has been doing in recent years, financial market participants invariably begin to wonder if inflation is rising. Since climbing gold prices have been a reliable indicator of inflation for millennia, the question of whether central banks are doing their jobs is inevitably raised, the ultimate professional insult for men like Fed Chairman Ben Bernanke or European Central Bank President Jean-Claude Trichet. By continually dumping gold on the market, the precious metal's price is artificially contained and this helps reduce concerns about inflation. Unfortunately, the falling amount of gold central banks hold is limited and cannot be replaced as easily as paper currency reserves without alerting the market. Unlike printing money, monetary decision-makers can't sell gold forever.

Over the last five years, central banks have contributed an average 14 percent of the annual gold supply in the market, which last year exceeded $10 billion. Though net accumulators of gold up until 1964, when central banks had amassed a combined 1.2 billion troy ounces of the precious metal, over the last four decades they have reduced their investments in bullion down to the present 850 million ounces, a 60-year low.[6] (See Figure 15.3.) The United States remains the most significant exception to gold selling, being the world's largest owner possessing almost a third of all gold reserves—8,135 tons worth roughly $177 billion. Perhaps the U.S. government has avoided selling gold (even though it might be lending some to bullion banks) out of concern about the attention it would immediately draw: This would signal that U.S. authorities were growing worried about the falling value of the dollar and perhaps precipitate an even faster decline.

Being such large owners (holding 18 percent of all existing gold in their vaults), central banks have kept gold prices steady by restricting their sales to an amount set under Central Bank Gold Agreements, much to the relief of the mining industry. Under the latest agreement, its 16 signatories (mostly European nations) are permitted to sell no more than 500 metric tons of gold each year.[7]

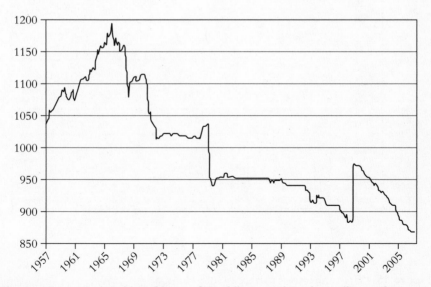

Figure 15.3   Total Gold Holdings of World's Central Banks (millions of ounces)
Source: IMF.

But in the last two years, to the surprise of many precious metals market observers, central banks have not been meeting their quota: For undisclosed reasons, monetary authorities in many countries have reduced their gold sales. Perhaps out of concern for the declining value of the dollar, in 2007 Germany, the world's fourth largest gold holder, surprised the market with the announcement that it would not be selling any gold in that year, and several other central banks had been reducing sales, as well. Meanwhile, smaller central banks, like those of Greece and the Philippines, have actually started buying gold, according to IMF figures.[8] But rumbling in the gold market regarding central bank moves had started two years before, when gold was still below $500 an ounce. In November of 2005, an official from Russia's central bank surprisingly said that it might double its gold reserves. Though holding a relatively small amount—about 500 tons, representing five percent of Russia's reserves at the time—the announcement caused a wave of speculation that contributed to gold's breaking $500, $600 and eventually $700 a few months later.[9] There was also mounting speculation about when Asian central banks, which hold miniscule gold holdings despite their soaring reserves, would finally begin accumulating bullion. (See Figure 15.4.)

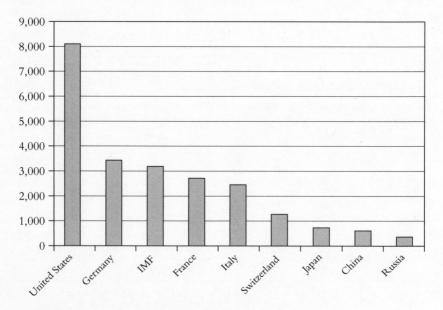

Figure 15.4   Countries with Largest Gold Holdings (in tons)
SOURCE: World Gold Council.

Gold might have also gained due to persistent rumors of a potential short squeeze in which gold players, having borrowed gold and sold it expecting a price decline, would be forced to buy back at higher prices, thereby driving bullion up even higher. Central banks have long been criticized in the gold trading world for creating a large short position in the market by lending sizeable amounts at low rates to bullion banks, like Goldman Sachs and J.P. Morgan Chase, though it is unclear how much is out on loan at any given time. One concern, formally raised before Congress by the Gold Anti-Trust Action Committee (GATA) in 2000, is that through this practice central banks manipulate gold prices and hence interfere with the proper functioning of financial markets. In April 2007, Peter Hambro, head of the British gold mining company that carries his name, expressed concern that the Bank of England may have lost control of the "small amount" of gold still left in its vaults due to this practice.[10] If, as GATA claims, between one-third and one-half of central bank holdings have been loaned out—regardless of their motivations—this could further limit what monetary authorities will be able to sell in the future, and puts further pressure on supply.

While central banks may be limiting sales partly for voluntary reasons, this is not true of the mining industry. Miners' supply of gold reached 2,621 tons in 2001 and has not reached that level since. South African production peaked in 1970 at close to 1,000 tons and has been falling continuously for over three decades. Weak gold prices in the late 1990s are explained in part by massive Australian mine production in that decade which peaked in 1997, and that of the U.S., which reached its highest in 1998.[11] But both countries' production is down substantially since then, and rising supplies from China and Latin America have not been sufficient to compensate. Although some research firms, like BMO of Canada, expect the wave of new investment in gold mines to boost gold production above the 2001 peak, others, like J.P. Morgan are skeptical because no new large deposits have been discovered.[12]

But even if mining supply recovers to 2001 levels, the cost of extracting and refining an ounce of gold has soared due to rising costs as well as the increasing difficulty of finding it. The average global cost of producing an ounce of gold has surged to nearly $500 an ounce, almost double the level of 2000. To maintain production at the South African Savuka (which means "rise up") deposit, miners work at a depth of 2.4 miles just to get 20 cubic centimeters out of a cubic meter of rock—that's just 20 parts per million by volume.[13] As mining costs continue climbing, only higher gold prices will justify new exploration to reach the ever-harder to extract deposits around the world. GFMS, the world's foremost precious metals consultancy, estimates that there are still 49,000 ounces of gold underground, many of which would need prices substantially higher than today's for them to be extracted profitably.

Though central banks have reduced sales and miners struggle to raise production, demand for gold continues to increase around the world driven by jewelry, industrial use and investment demand. Jewelry represents 68 percent of annual consumption, about 2,300 tons each year, and $44 billion in gold jewelry purchases were made around the world in 2006.[14] The growing affluence of consumers throughout Asia, most notably in India and China, have increased purchases, and a weakening dollar has made prices in their currencies rise more modestly than they have in the United States.

Although demand has grown in many countries, India remains, by far, the world's largest consumer of gold, accounting for 22 percent of global jewelry demand and 35 percent of all bullion coins and bars. The country buys one and a half times more gold each year than the United States, the second largest consumer.[15] While gold demand is an important part of cultural and religious traditions dating from thousands of years ago, the most significant driver of Indian gold consumption has been the country's economic boom. The surge in outsourcing and information technology jobs has raised the standard of living for millions of skilled Indian workers that are demanding higher and higher wages. Economic forecasting agency Global Insight expects the number of people earning between $13,000–30,000, $30,000–80,000 and over $80,000 to increase by 52 percent, 87 percent and 200 percent in real terms to 167 million, 30 million, and 3 million workers respectively by 2015.[16] Another important source of Indian demand comes from the rural community, home to 70 percent of the population, which has traditionally used gold as a secure form of savings.

China, the world's third largest consumer of gold, is a step behind India and the United States in demand partly because citizens were prohibited from owning the precious metal in any form until 1982. And until 2007, only professional traders were able to buy and sell gold bullion, as individuals were forced to purchase via investment funds or to pay higher prices for physical gold through jewelry and coins. The Shanghai Gold Exchange launched individual gold bullion trading nationwide in July 2007, a move that is expected to be an important source of future demand.[17] While Gold turnover at the exchange reached 1,249 tons in 2006, a 38 percent gain from the previous year, the new demand from individuals that will finally be able to buy bullion at more attractive prices could be a tremendous driver of gold prices. The average Chinese worker saves over 40 percent of his or her take-home pay, the highest savings rate in the world. Now that there is increasing concern about the skyrocketing Chinese stock market and real estate bubbles popping, perhaps the Chinese will begin accumulating gold more quickly than they have been doing already.

Of the roughly 4,000 tons of gold that miners, central banks and scrap sellers place on the market each year, 16 percent is destined toward investment demand. This is the gold that ends up being melted into gold bars, coins and medals of many kinds that are bought by individual investors, precious metals funds of various kinds and exchange-traded funds, a completely new source of investment demand.

Exchange-traded gold funds for the first time allow international investors to buy and sell gold bullion for their investment accounts without actually needing to store it. Launched first on the New York Stock Exchange in 2004, there are now seven active gold ETFs listed on nine stock exchanges across the world.[18] Transaction costs are extremely low, and investors are assured that all the ETF securities are backed by gold held in a vault on behalf of investors. The ability to finally buy gold, pure and simple, and not some gold fund invested at the whim of a portfolio manager at high account management fees, has been a significant driver of gold demand in just the last two years, as gold ETFs had amassed 648 tons of gold by the end of 2006.[19] Like the individual gold trading accounts that were recently authorized on the Shanghai Gold Exchange in China, gold ETFs are a completely new source of demand for gold, and there are plans to launch them on several other exchanges around the world—perhaps most importantly in India—over the next two years.

Part Five

HOW TO BUY GOLD

Chapter 16

When You Simply Want Financial Insurance

I f you have decided to buy gold, there are a several ways to go about investing in the precious metal, and doing so has become easier than ever thanks mostly to the Internet. This chapter answers some basic questions about investing in physical gold bullion. Bullion simply refers to refined gold that is at least 99.5 percent pure, often in the form of bars, wafers, ingots, or coins that lack the numismatic value of rare coins. I prefer buying gold bullion in coin form such as an American Eagle, South African Kruggerand, or Canadian Maple Leaf, which cost about the same, per ounce, as the dull bars and are strikingly beautiful, as you can see in Figure 16.1. Most are minted in 22-karat gold, though some, like the recently released American Buffalo are made of 24-karat gold of 99.99 percent purity.

The next chapter considers the advantages and disadvantages of owning gold indirectly via mining stocks, ETFs, and through an innovative

Figure 16.1   American Eagle Coin

currency known as digital gold. Chapter 18 considers what I regard as a very aggressive way to profit from rising gold prices—the rare coin market. Going out on a speculative limb, if gold surges as I and many others anticipate, I believe that the rare coin market could become the next '90s Nasdaq. Today, as I write in 2007, I believe there are few things that offer the combination of ultimate investment security and conservative potential for profit of gold bullion stored in a safe at the bank. But for the ambitious investor who is willing to assume some degree of risk for the potential of large long-term returns, rare coins are a hidden investment class worth considering—and an American rare coin index has outperformed the Dow Jones Industrial Average over the last six decades, as discussed in Chapter 18.

There are other ways to invest in gold using the derivatives markets or taking advantage of financial leverage, but I will avoid discussing this manner of investing here. Though the experienced investor may prefer to own gold via the futures market, which is practical, safe and cost-effective,

I think of gold as something one should generally own in physical form. Gold is the ultimate escape from financial risk. It has proven itself to be the most widely accepted store of value during all times of economic turmoil, especially when the value of paper currencies has become highly uncertain, as I believe it will be in the years immediately ahead. I think gold should be a part, large or small, of all portfolios, large or small. But I suggest applying investment gymnastics to other types of traded assets in increasingly volatile financial markets, and to think of gold as an investment outside your brokerage account, as a simple, trusted store of value that you can hold in your hands, where it will be entirely under your control.

How Much Gold Should I Own?

If I were to recommend that you hold no more than 5 percent of your wealth in gold in a traditional diversified portfolio dominated by stocks, as a typical financial advisor would, you would not believe me. The previous chapters show my deep concern that we are entering troublesome times of financial turmoil and substantially more than 5 percent of my personal assets are in gold and silver (another precious metal I will discuss in Chapter 19). But that does not mean there is no risk in holding gold. I've made an argument that gold will rise sharply in the years ahead, a view I hold with conviction, though not certainty. Unless you can predict the future, you should always maintain some degree of diversification across financial asset classes. Finding the right percentage of gold to own is something you should consider carefully.

In discussing gold with a financial advisor, you are likely to be met with deep skepticism. I face it often among the highly-trained and experienced financial experts with whom I work and with the Wall Street traders, analysts, economists and strategists I speak and correspond with by e-mail. Invariably you will find a recurring argument against gold is that it cannot be modeled: there is no proven way to predict with any certainty how much gold will rise or fall next year. It's just so unpredictable, so erratic. However, could we not say the same thing about the stock market, which once went down 20 percent in a single day? Had that been "modeled"? Gold has never fallen that sharply. Had the present turmoil in the credit markets that has forced several hedge funds and over 50 mortgage brokers—including the largest—to shut down been modeled? Several money market funds, which are considered by most to be as safe as cash, fell more than 10 percent in July, 2007, and I can't imagine a financial model that would have predicted that. (Has it ever happened before?) What has certainly been modeled is that a broker, trader, or financial advisor cannot earn any trading or account management fees, much less make poor investment decisions on your behalf with an asset sitting securely in your safe deposit box at the bank.★ Think about that for a minute.

When deciding how much gold to own, you should always keep in mind the effect this will have on your overall portfolio. This is of vital importance, particularly if you are nearing retirement. If you will need to sell part of your gold in less than a few months, it is probably a better idea to keep that portion of your money in cash. I am in contact with some persons who get overly excited about gold and can't wait to buy more, much like many stock market investors were in the late '90s. Don't fall into this "the financial world is going to collapse" trap and suddenly realize the world has not stopped rotating and that you rely entirely on the fate of gold to determine your future. Also keep in mind that gold does not pay dividends or interest and that, as with other financial assets, you must pay taxes on any gains you make.

Considering present financial conditions, I would suggest holding eight to 15 percent of your financial assets in gold and I would not think it insane to hold as much as 50 percent. But just keep in mind that once you get over, say, 20 percent of your assets in gold you are expressing the conviction—with me—that gold will outperform other financial assets over the next few years, which is educated speculation. Even if you share my deep concerns, don't think you are being "conservative" by concentrating your assets in gold. If the $115-billion Teacher Retirement System of Texas that I work for moved 30 percent of its assets into gold, this would be highly imprudent and our chief investment officer would likely be fired and rightly so. No matter what the financial environment is, concentrating investment in a single asset class is always a risky

---

★Safety deposit boxes are extremely cheap to rent these days, perhaps a reflection of the fact that few people store wealth in hard assets anymore. You can rent one at the downtown offices of Chase in Austin, Texas, for less than $50 a year.

proposition. However, I think we are living in extraordinary times. I believe the risks in other asset classes, like stocks and bonds, are so high that I have moved away from them and concentrated *my* investments in precious metals. This is a personal risk I decided to assume because I think it is the best way to protect my family's assets today.

What Should I Own?

If you are looking for physical gold, just bullion, here is a simple rule of thumb: Look for a gold product whose price is not far from the spot price of gold in the market, the one you see listed in a newspaper's financial section. If the newspaper or Yahoo! Finance website shows the ounce of gold to have closed at $680 and you can buy an ounce at $700 (a 3 percent premium), that is a reasonable price for a purchase of at least four ounces of gold. (A slightly higher premium would probably be needed if you are buying just an ounce or two, or if you want some of the more popular bullion coins, like American Eagles. A lower mark-up should be expected for large orders.) The premium reflects the multiple costs a gold dealer incurs to sell it to you, and is probably making virtually no profit on the low volume transaction. Often he or she just hopes that giving you a good price will encourage you to become his or her client when you make additional purchases in the future, which is reasonable.

Aside from gold bars, which are usually sold very near the price of gold in the market, South African Kruggerands are generally the cheapest (lowest premium over the spot price of gold on the market) of bullion coins and American Eagles and Buffalos are among the most expensive. This because they are the most desirable in the largest retail market for the trading of bullion gold coins in the world, which is the United States. Many countries mint gold coins every year, and I think some of the most beautiful are Chinese Pandas, Austrian Philarmonics, and Australian Kangaroos, all of which can be bought at prices that will generally be less than four percent above raw gold prices in the market. (See Figure 16.2.) Since most of these bullion coins cost about the same and are easy to buy and sell, get the ones you like the most.

I try to stay away from gold products offered in TV or mass circulation ads and buying from individuals over the Internet. How rare or unique can be something sold on the television or offered to millions of

Figure 16.2　The Australian Nugget Coin

readers? (No further discussion is required!) I have heard several stories of buyers getting ripped off by purchasing from persons selling gold on Ebay, either because a rare coin had been misgraded or because a gold product received was not precisely what had been advertised. That being said, the large number of products being offered on Ebay implies that many gold items are being traded over the website. But unless you have guidance from someone that has successfully bought and sold gold on Ebay, I would avoid buying gold from anybody other than an established, reputable gold dealer.

I also steer clear of once-in-a-lifetime precious metal opportunities in general. If a gold salesperson or website tells you of some uniquely valuable gold coin or medal, such as a coin commemorating the 60th anniversary of the end of World War II or Mickey Mouse's birthday, which is priced more than 10 percent above its gold content, I hope you truly love it. Because if you don't and decide to sell it in a few years you are likely to hear a dreaded word from a potential buyer at a coin shop: melt. Coins, medals, or bars that are not uniquely desirable in the marketplace—the large physical marketplace where hundreds of different coins and items made of gold are exchanged—will be bought at melt, meaning based solely on their gold content. If gold were trading at $680 an ounce and you bought an ounce coin for $782 (at a 15 percent premium for the once-in-a-lifetime opportunity) and decided to turn around and sell it, you would probably get $680 for it . . . less a charge for taking the coin to the gold scrap shop, where all the other unforgettable events are forgotten. You would lose at least a hundred dollars. As I'll discuss in the rare coin section, I think this approach makes sense if you are buying gold as an investment: unless you are Bill Gates, buy gold thinking you (or a relative or an heir) will probably want to sell it some day. You should try to buy gold in a form that will be relatively easy to sell (like a bullion gold American Eagle or MS-64 $10 Liberty gold coin from the late 1800s) because it is very well known and popular. (You'll understand what MS-64 means after reading Chapter 18 on rare coins.)

If you are buying new issues from the U.S. Mint or other mints around the world, remember that today's bullion coins are tomorrow's rare coins and that their value is higher when preserved scratchless in the box or sleeve in which you receive them. (If you are rich and want to use gold coins as poker chips, then you probably don't need to read this paragraph.) A flawless coin will generally be more valuable than a damaged one, especially if it is certified as being virtually perfect. (More on certification in Chapter 18.) Although most precious metals coins minted in the last twenty years or so have not acquired "numismatic" value that would separate them from other bullion coins, keep in mind that a great many Americans—somewhere between 1.3 to 1.8 million serious collectors in the country—are continuously forming collections, so there will always be a need for key year coins that can become scarce.[1] So, in time, some of the more desirable coins will gradually appreciate more than others, and none will rise more than the flawless ones. Not that you have 87 years of patience, but consider that the 1920 $10 Indian Head gold coin sold by Dr. Steven Duckor in March 2007 for $1,725,000 was once a bullion coin.[2]

What Is the Best Way to Go about Buying Physical Gold and Not Get Ripped Off?

There has never been an easier time to buy gold with confidence than today, thanks to reliable physical delivery systems and the Internet. Much of the physical gold purchased in the United States today is done so in cyberspace, where a great many precious metals businesses small and large compete. Type "buy gold" in your web search engine and the number of gold products offered will make you dizzy. Much like purchasing a book on Amazon.com, once you have found a trustworthy gold dealer, you can buy hundreds of thousands, if not millions of dollars in gold online and have the precious acquisition insured and mailed to you with confidence that the investment will arrive safely. Crazy as it sounds to *mail* gold, consider the win-win coin toss implied in over-insuring: If you mail $10,000 in gold but insure it for $12,000, heads you get your $10,000 in gold, tails you get $12,000 in cash.

A great many millions of dollars in gold are mailed across the United States every year, though these precious packages are generally insured and labeled in a way that do not give away the contents. And a million dollars in gold would probably not be sent in a single package! I bought some of my first gold, Swiss Helvetia coins from the 1920s, over the Internet and I nervously waited—and repeatedly phoned the firm that sold me the gold—for the postal card telling me I could pick the package up at the post office. Since then, I have sent and received a great many golden parcels across the country—always cautiously packaging and fully insuring each one—and have yet to face a problem other than a delay.

Any business that involves money attracts sleazy people that will try to rip you off, and the gold business is no exception. There are several shops—some well-known in the precious metals dealer community—that take advantage of novices who are perhaps nervously buying gold for the first time, and these firms pray on their clients' vulnerability. Here's an example: During the summer of 2006, the U.S. Mint released an eagerly-awaited new gold coin, the American Buffalo, the first U.S. coin minted in 24-karat gold (the previous ones had been 22-karat). A lot of excitement was generated by the release, and many new buyers, fearing the newly issued coins could get away from them forever, forgot the simple truth that the coin was still just an ounce of gold and that tens of thousands of them would be minted. With these coins being worth less than $750 each, there was a particular shop that was offering them openly, on the Internet, at $2,000 each. Today, as I write in the summer of 2007, you can buy this same coin easily over the Internet, day or night, in certified flawless condition for under $1,000 . . . or cheaper by the dozen! Buying gold is often like buying a car: Even brilliant men and women with PhDs can be turned into suckers. Remember that there is always a place for you to get ripped off legally, and the gold business is no exception.

Use the Internet to your advantage in two ways. First, choose a gold dealer with whom you can establish a relationship of trust and try to find an individual there that has been at the firm for at least a few years. If you don't feel comfortable talking with him or her for any reason, speak to someone else! A solid gold dealer can steer you away from bad deals and direct you toward potentially profitable ones. They want you to profit because your disappointment will make them lose your business. A good place to start looking is to find an authorized dealer with the Professional Coin Grading Service (www.pcgs.com) or the Numismatic Guaranty Corporation (ngccoin.com) listed on their websites. See if the dealer's website reveals the number of years the company has been operating, with less than 10 years possibly being a concern. Their website should reveal if they belong to the local Better Business Bureau, which I think is an indispensable requirement.

Second, once you have determined what you are going to buy, get a price from your dealer and check it on the Internet. By Googling the precise product you are buying, like a 2005 American Eagle one-ounce gold coin, you can quickly find out what price you could pay by shopping elsewhere. If you find that you could buy the coin for a few dollars less at another, perhaps less trustworthy shop, it might not be worth the trouble, but if substantially more were involved, then you might ask your dealer if he or she can match the lower price. They might not be able to beat the price, but then you will need to consider the confidence you have in the other dealer you've found on the Web. As with any purchase, be wary of prices that are too low, which might be a sign of trouble. Once you've decided to go ahead with your first acquisition with a new shop, you might want to start with a small purchase, perhaps using the company's website for an electronic transaction, and see how smoothly the process goes.

The physical gold market really is a market: You can haggle! If you don't like a price, say so! But keep something in mind. Gold dealers are used to dealing in high dollar amounts, and even if they are handling a $100 order for a person of modest means, this may have been after discussing a $500,000 deal with another client. If you are buying two bullion gold coins (a transaction under $2,000), don't think you are smart in gaining five dollars from the dealer after imploring her or him for a better deal. You may feel wiser for making a few bucks, but by annoying the dealer, you will probably be called last when he or she gets notice of a desirable new shipment of gold or silver coins that are likely to fly. Keep in mind that, when the gold market heats up, you could find yourself begging for attention at that understaffed—as they all tend to be—shop, so best to make a friend. I'd suggest driving a bargain when it is worth it. A dealer will respect you for trying to get a fair deal, but don't waste precious time over five bucks.

You can save money on your precious metals purchases by talking with a person instead of buying online. Quite often the 24-hour prices you see on websites for Internet orders are not the lowest you will be able to find. To protect themselves against an overnight rise in the price of gold (something happening more and more often), dealers often list prices that are slightly higher than they would offer over the phone. Call a gold shop and try to get a better price, which most of the time you will. Like in most businesses, a gold dealer will not want to disappoint you, knowing you have many other places to buy gold thanks to the glory of the Internet. This might expose you to an undesirable conversation with a person that would like to sell you more, but with a "Thanks, I'm not interested in anything else," you could save yourself a lot of money.

Other than choosing the wrong gold dealer, the biggest mistake you can make is to fall into the urgency trap. Like autos at the car lot, precious metals products often seem to be "running out" or prices about to rise "like crazy," and the coin you are interested in might be getting away from you. But, alas, they are still there tomorrow and next week . . . unless the precious metals market is hot! When gold broke $500 and kept going past $600 in early 2006, dealer inventories were being depleted, prices were rising insanely (especially rare coins) and coins were getting away from buyers. But if at the time you are buying the market is relatively stable, be patient. Hang up the phone or step away from your computer and think about it before buying anything.

Chapter 17

Mining Stocks, ETFs, and GoldMoney

Should I Invest in Gold via Mining Stocks?

Not long ago, a friend suggested investing in gold mining stocks since they had not been rising faster than gold. As of the writing of these lines, gold had risen more than the Philadelphia Gold & Silver Index (XAU) for three years, the former rising 66 percent, and the latter 58 percent (including dividends). And technical stock market observers of the XAU have been pointing out that when gold outperforms components of the index continuously, it is time to buy the stocks. In a gold bull market, stocks often rise ahead of the precious metal since they are, in some ways, a call option on gold. This means that when gold begins to rise, gold stocks—especially the ones that have abundant reserves ready to be exploited—will climb faster in value. However, in recent years, this has not happened. Why?

Most mining companies are struggling to increase production and costs are climbing very rapidly due to rising labor costs, higher prices, more shortages of energy, increasing taxes and royalties, as well as the sheer difficulty, quite simply, of digging deeper to extract the scarce precious metal. Ore grades at some important mining operations across the world have continued to decline.[1] Mining giant Newmont reported disappointing earnings in May 2007 due to soaring energy and other costs. Expenses at one of its Nevada mines jumped from $395 to nearly $500 an ounce of gold in just one year.[2] As a result of surging costs, gold mining industry earnings—the dominant driver of stock prices—have been disappointing. Thus, despite their exposure to climbing gold prices, mining stocks carry many of the same uncertainties that other stocks do, like rising costs. An additional risk is that many mining operations are in distant nations where fickle governments can change the rules of the game. Governments can raise taxes, interfere in operations or nationalize or outright confiscate mining operations. Should their profits rise dramatically in a gold bull market, which might accompany a weak economy, leaders could feel justified in trying to confiscate some of those profits. It has certainly happened before.

Notwithstanding these concerns, investing in mining stocks can often help a gold investor gain more than he or she would have earned through buying gold alone; in fact this is often the case. Buying individual stocks can be exciting and highly rewarding, especially the smaller mining plays that can double, triple and more on news of a new gold deposit discovery or their being taken over by a larger company. But if you decide to move away from conservatively-run mining companies with diversified operations around the world like Barrick, AngloGold and Newmont to invest in small cap speculative mining stocks, let me tell you about Bre-X.

That the history of gold mining is replete with stories of deception is evident in Mark Twain's cynical observation that "A gold mine is a hole in the ground with a liar on top."[3] Twain would have laughed at the story of Bre-X, a corporate scandal that rocked the gold mining world in the 1990s.[4] For the sake of brevity, let me give you the highlights of this cautionary tale. Bre-X began as an obscure Calgary gold exploration company with no revenues or earnings. Its executives, having searched for gold unsuccessfully in the far-off jungles of Kalimantan, Indonesia, decided to say that they had actually found rich deposits. In time, providing false earth samples that gullible investment analysts trusted, Bre-X went from estimating deposits of 3 million ounces of gold to *two hundred million*, which at the time amounted to 70 billion dollars for an asset the company didn't even have a clear title to. Wall Street ate this up—salivating for each of the many lies Bre-X management continually fed it—and a great many analysts promoted the stock relentlessly, some saying they "had seen the gold" with their own eyes. In what we might call its Microsoft phase, Bre-X went from trading at pennies per share to a peak of $286.50 in 1996, when it reached a stunning market capitalization of $6 billion. Its Enron phase, during which a Bre-X executive en route to explain why there was no gold dove to his death from a helicopter, ended with the stock recording a final trade at seven cents a share.

Episodes like the Bre-X scandal are evidently rare, but keep in mind that gold has a way of attracting swindlers that prey on investors' ever-present desire for fast profits. Unless you plan to immerse yourself into the world of mining stocks, it would be best to invest in some of the gold "seniors" mentioned above, the large, well-managed companies that generally have solid balance sheets and relatively stable earnings—at least as far as mining companies go. For the investor that doesn't have hours to spend on finding the ideal stock or set of stocks, there are several gold stock indices that have given rise to exchange-traded funds of mining companies. Most major investment companies also have gold and/or precious metals funds that invest in a basket of mining companies around the world.

Should I Buy Gold Using an Exchange-Traded Fund?

Exchange-traded gold funds have been a major driver of investment demand since they began trading in late 2004, just a few years ago. Under the symbol "GLD," State Street Global Advisors (the world's largest institutional money manager) and the World Gold Council launched the first gold-based security backed by a representative portion of physical gold bullion held in a secure vault. As more investors buy GLD shares, the fund's managers are obligated to accumulate the equivalent dollar amount in gold bullion. For the first time, investors wary of holding physical gold due to inconvenience or other reasons can gain secure and

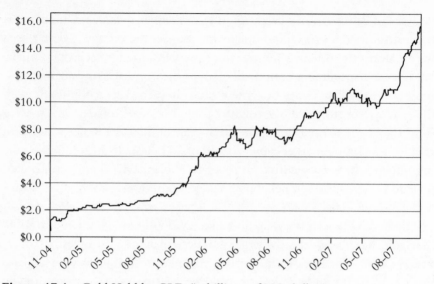

Figure 17.1   Gold Held by GLD (in billions of U.S. dollars)
SOURCE: exchangetradedfund.com.

cost-effective access to the precious metal and trade it, for the first time, like any liquid stock. In addition to the New York–listed gold ETF, there are gold ETFs listed in London, Sydney and Johannesburg. GLD can also be traded on several other European exchanges, as well as on the Singapore and Mexican Stock Exchanges, and there are plans for gold to be traded on virtually all exchanges relatively soon. Holding over $13 billion in gold (see Figure 17.1), gold ETFs in time will allow much of the world's investors to buy gold more conveniently than ever before.

With $1.9 trillion under management, State Street Global Advisors handles more wealth than most of the world's countries and is perhaps the strongest foundation upon which a gold ETF could have been launched. Although some gold "purists" might argue that part of the gold might not actually be physically held by State Street, but rather in the form of derivatives (since one cannot peek in the vault), I doubt the World Gold Council would allow this. The win–win objective of gold ETFs was to make it easier for buyers to acquire gold, on the one hand, and to boost physical demand to the benefit of the gold mining industry, on the other. Since the tons of gold that underlie GLD shares are revealed at the end of each trading day, State Street offers more transparency on its holding than the U.S. federal government.

Gold ETFs are a safe, cost-effective and easy way to acquire gold. But here is a potential problem that may seem improbable today, but which is important to consider for investors concerned about ultimate investment safety, which is, after all, the main reason to own gold: World governments in time may decide to change the rules of the game and force gold ETFs, less than a decade old, to delist.

Consider this scenario, unlikely as it may seem at first glance: A disaster occurs, monetary or otherwise, and investors flock to gold ETFs—instead of cash, as many would have before ETFs were around. The sudden demand for listed gold—which is now, after all, just a mouse click away for investors in trillions of assets around the world—would force gold ETF managers to pull substantial gold tonnage off the global commodities markets leading to a massive spike in the price of gold. This could conceivably intensify into a tidal wave of investment out of other financial markets and into gold, a move that the hedge funds that today manage over a trillion dollars would be sure to take advantage of. This would be immensely disruptive to the global financial system and perhaps take a significant portion of paper money, the essential tool that central bankers use to regulate the world economy, out of circulation by leaps and bounds.

At that point, world governments could feel justified in reaching what would be a fairly simply decision: Shut down the ETFs. Gold would have to be purchased the old-fashioned way, but the turmoil would likely draw even more attention to the scarcity and investment value of the precious metal, probably making physical gold even more attractive to investors, and hence more costly. But what gold would you, as an investor, hold after ETFs suspended operations? The ETF would send you a check in the mail or credit to your brokerage account in dollars. You would not receive a physical delivery of gold because you never actually owned any. You owned a piece of paper that represented an investment in gold. To consider that something like this may happen could seem extreme, but one owns gold to deal with extreme situations.

What Is Digital Gold Currency and How Can I Use It?

Whereas gold ETFs allow investors to own a representative amount of gold, there is now a way to invest in the precious metal by owning actual physical gold secured in a vault and be able to use it like money. Today there are financial institutions that serve as digital vaults of their clients' gold, which they can use as a currency to carry out online commerce just as they would with any bank. The amount of gold stored in this way is growing rapidly as monetary uncertainty grows.

After several start-ups and a few failures, GoldMoney, which today stores over $200 million of gold and silver for its clients, has emerged as the world's premier digital gold financial institution. Like an international online bank, through its website goldmoney.com GoldMoney accepts major currencies, which its customers can immediately convert into units of physical gold, called the goldgram, which is a gram of gold. Gold is then stored in a bullion vault near London or another in Zurich, Switzerland. Clients wanting to diversify away from their paper currency holdings can simply hold gold and silver at GoldMoney conveniently, or use the gold in their accounts to make payments back into paper currencies online. Unlike gold certificates and ETFs, the precious metal held at GoldMoney is not simply representative: If needed, clients can request an actual withdrawal of their physical gold bullion, which would be insured and shipped to them directly.

Skeptical potential account openers might show concern they cannot see the actual gold held on their behalf, much less hold it in their hands, just as I cannot see the actual money held in my bank account. I simply trust that it is there because I am 99 percent confident that I can withdraw money on demand. In the early 1980s, International Gold Bullion Exchange, once the largest gold bullion dealer in the United States, shocked thousands of customers when it was discovered that gold bars in the company's vault were actually made of wood. Tens of millions of dollars were lost.[5]

To overcome this concern, when James Turk founded GoldMoney he concentrated on setting up solid guarantees for the financial institution's clients. To begin with, he encouraged two of the most respected mining companies, DRDGOLD of South Africa and IAMGOLD of Canada, to become core shareholders. Secondly, he insured all the gold and silver, which meet the standards of the "chain of integrity" of the London Bullion Market Association, through a policy underwritten by Lloyd's of London. And perhaps most importantly, he ensured the integrity of the gold and silver with regular audits by one of the world's four largest accounting firms. To prevent political interference with its clients' right to own gold—which was, after all, confiscated from citizens by the U.S. government in 1933—GoldMoney was established in Jersey, in the British Channel Islands, which has a centuries-old tradition of respecting property rights.

Though it seemed ahead of its time a few years ago, the growing amount of gold and silver stored by its clients at GoldMoney shows that confidence in digital gold currency is growing rapidly. At the end of June 2007, GoldMoney held 6.3 tons of gold and 4.3 million ounces of silver, amounts that were 24 percent and 65 percent higher, respectively, than in 2006. Aside from the fact that gold is used as its currency, perhaps what most distinguishes the financial institution from banks is that money received is not lent out, which would create a liability for GoldMoney: money sent to the financial institution is converted into goldgrams, nothing more. GoldMoney simply stores gold and offers easy, liquid access to it. Nothing more, nothing less.

Gold is an asset that has a proven history of adding diversification benefits to any traditional investment portfolio of stocks, bonds, and other assets. What this means, in essence, is that gold generally has the advantage of not going down—and often rising in value—when other asset values fall. Table 17.1 lists what I believe are the nine main ways of investing in the precious metal for readers that are interested in the subtleties of owning gold. I have listed the nine ways ranging from mining stocks to jewelry, dividing them into three groups: "paper gold" (like gold ETFs), physical gold, and "in between," listing the pros and cons of each manner of investing. Each of them is ranked based on my personal opinion of its ultimate investment safety and potential, as well as its liquidity (the ease with which you can buy and sell it).

The reader will also find that I included a column in which I grade each way of investing based on "government risk," the possibility that our leaders could interfere with the free and unimpeded ownership of gold and begin to regulate its possession at some time in the future. Though considering such a risk may appear naïve in these prosperous times, gold regulation and outright confiscation are not without precedent in our history. And a gold investor is often concerned with all risks, remote as some may seem today.

Table 17.1 Ways to Own Gold

			Pros	Cons	Investment Safety	Investment Potential	Liquidity	Government Risk	Score
PAPER GOLD	**In between**	**PHYSICAL GOLD**							
1 Mining Stocks			• Can rise faster than gold or silver • Very easy to buy and sell	• No gold under your physical control • Many of same risks attached to other stocks • Costs of mining gold climbing fast	3	4	5	4	16
2 Commodity Futures			• Very easy to buy and sell • Can take delivery of physical gold • Highly liquid	• Risk of regulatory change affecting use	4	3	5	1	13
3 Gold Certificates			• Represents gold ownership • Easy to convert to cash in most cases	• No gold under your physical control • You are allowing a bank to owe you something	2	3	4	1	10
4 ETFs			• Very easy to buy and sell • Represents gold ownership • Highly liquid	• No gold under your physical control • Risk of government interference	4	3	5	1	13
5	GoldMoney		• Very easy to buy and sell • Gold is actually owned • Highly liquid	• Gold is owned, but stored by 3rd. Party • Though gold is not lent, requires trust in mgmt.	4	3	5	5	17
6		Gold Bullion Coins/Bars	• Relatively easy to buy and sell • Gold is owned/in physical possession	• Need to personally store	5	3	4	1	13

#		Description	Investment Safety	Investment Potential	Liquidity	Government Risk	Score
7	**Gold "Common Date" Coins**	• Can rise faster than gold or silver • Historically has outperformed stocks • Gold is owned/in physical possession	• Not easy to sell quickly • Down market periods can be deep, lengthy • Need to personally store	5	5	3	5	18
8	**Rare Coins**	• Can rise faster than gold or silver • Historically has outperformed stocks • Gold is owned/in physical possession	• Not easy to sell quickly • Down market periods can be deep, lengthy • Need to personally store	5	5	2	5	17
9	**Jewelry**	• Gold is owned/in physical possession • Fashionable/ aesthetically pleasing	• Likely to redeem only fraction of gold value • Not easy to sell quickly	5	2	1	5	13

Scale: 1 to 5, 5 is highest.

These numbers are based on the judgement of the author. I would not suggest buying gold based on the best score, but rather based on what fits a reader's individual needs. For example, if you do not believe government risk is a concern, then bullion, commodity futures, and gold certificates would be more attractive than the score above implies. Keep in mind that gold should be considered a long-term investment that adds diversification benefits to a portfolio.

Investment Safety refers to ultimate safety, meaning which is safest in conditions of extreme financial stress. Hence, this is not an issue in normal conditions. Safety is low for mining stocks because of equity market and operational risks.

It is low for gold certificates because these are ultimately pieces of paper that are another party's liability. It is high for physical gold, being outside of paper financial markets, yet it suffers from low liquidity.

Investment Potential: 3 means the asset will rise or fall in line with the market price of gold. 4 or 5 indicates the probability that the asset would rise more than gold or silver (or fall more in a precious metals bear market). Jewelry was rated 2 because it will typically be bought at or below melt (the price of gold in the market).

Liquidity refers to the ease of buying and selling the asset. Rare and common date coins score poorly because it is difficult to sell in a hurry. Jewelry might be easy to sell quickly, but at a very low price.

Government Risk: risk that government could change the rules of the game in gold ownership. (See Chapter 18 for discussion of this risk.) 5 means virtually no risk and 1 means high risk if the government decided (once again) to prohibit private ownership of gold. Mining stocks receive a 4 because, in periods of financial stress, their corporate tax rate could be raised, especially if gold prices were rising rapidly. GoldMoney is based away from the United States to prevent the possibility of government intervention in its management. Rare coins, gold and silver coins with numismatic value, have never been confiscated.

Score is based on a simple addition of the four factors.

Chapter 18

Rare Coins: A Bet on the Highest Possible Gains in Gold

All persons are hereby required to deliver on or before May 1, 1933, to a Federal Reserve Bank or branch or agency thereof or to any member bank of the Federal Reserve System all gold coin, gold bullion, and gold certificates.
PRESIDENT FRANKLIN DELANO ROOSEVELT, APRIL 5, 1933.[1]

I n one of the worst years of the Great Depression, the federal government required the great number of citizens taking financial refuge in gold to surrender it in exchange for Federal Reserve notes that were soon to be printed in large quantities. In the stroke of a pen, the White House withdrew the economic freedom implied in gold and decreed, in essence, that inflation would be created by force. What Alan Greenspan once referred to as the hidden confiscation of wealth had begun.[2]

The announcement came just weeks after Roosevelt's inauguration as well as a flurry of bank panics and holidays during which doors remained closed to the horror of depositors. It truly was horror. Literally thousands of banks across the country were collapsing as mobs of worried people ran them, hoping to recover their savings at a time when deposits were not government-insured, as they are today. And then the federal government, worried about a run on its own gold reserves and massive exports of gold to Europe, seemed to be taking away the last refuge for the public's wealth. Well, almost the last. Treasury Secretary William Woodin ensured, in the Gold Reserve Act of 1934, that coins with a "recognized special value to collectors of rare and unusual coin" be exempt from gold confiscation.[3]

It is for this reason that to this day gold dealers often refer to some gold products—all gold bullion, including coins—as "confiscatable" and others as "non-confiscatable" in reference to coins that have numismatic value, which is to say, rare coins. To make this distinction may seem quaint today, since American citizens have been allowed to own gold bullion since 1974, and the country's monetary system appears to be functioning as it should, despite surging debt levels, increasingly volatile financial markets, and a falling dollar. But in the future, if an economic calamity, such as a dollar crash, causes a global panic and surge of money out of paper currencies and into hard money, the government may once again force us out of gold. Confiscation risk is evidently very low today, but in the event of a sudden mass flight to gold—which would most certainly be a concern for government leaders—you would be wise to buy some rare coins. You would also be wise to buy them in normal times.

Since the 1940s, perhaps the highest possible long-term investment return in an index of any kind has been found in the American rare coins market. Two renowned rare coin experts, David Ganz and David Bowers, maintain rare coin indexes that have beat stocks by a wide margin for years. Ganz's rare coin index rose an average 13.7 percent per year between 1938 and 2004 compared with 8.4 percent for the Dow Jones Industrial Average and Bowers' has shown similar performance.[4] And considering that the Dow has been regularly pruned of poor performing stocks over the years, rare coins' outperformance is actually even stronger. In early 2006, a 1927 gold coin auctioned for $176,000 in 1982 was sold for $1.9 million.[5] But those lacking a million or two to spare have taken comfort in the fact that multiple other rare coins—a great many selling for under $5,000 today—rose during this period, as well, though less dramatically. There is a rare coin market at all price levels, and values have continued climbing during this decade, sometimes faster.

Several pre-1933 gold coins selling for under $1,000 in October 2005, like $10 gold Indian Head coins in a grade known as MS-63 (explained below), had doubled in value eight months later.

But the cost for such impressive performance is mostly patience. Coin prices typically rise in violent spurts over several months, as seen with the $10 gold Indian Head mentioned above, and then can remain dormant—or decline—over subsequent months. Since the rare coin market tends to move in cycles of four or five years under normal market conditions, that is often the time needed to show a healthy profit. Coin expert Scott Travers wrote that a holding period of ten years is ideal and I think many coin specialists would say two to three years is reasonable, making the rare coin market intensely unattractive to day-traders wanting to flip stocks for a fast profit.[6] Successful rare coin investors buy the best coins they can afford at reasonable prices and lock them away for years. This long holding period provides rare coin investors with high potential rewards, but a not-insignificant risk is the need to sell too soon at a loss. Rare coins are long term assets.

Absent today, there used to be an additional cost inherent in buying rare coins. Although the market was strong in the late 1960s and through-out the '70s, it was very difficult for novices to profit in the market because only experts knew how to compare the quality of different coins with precision to determine their value. While there has long been a widely accepted grading scale, evaluating any given coin was a highly subjective undertaking and what for one grader could be a $1,000 coin for another was worth $1,800. But since the mid-1980s, when widely respected institutions launched a new grading system, most well pre-served coins today are certified with quality and rarity recognized by virtually all coin dealers. In fact, a great many certified coins are traded sight unseen, meaning certified coins don't even need to be seen and held to be acknowledged as holding a defined value. The market has also become far more transparent thanks to the Internet, where buyers and sellers can look up prices and verify important information about virtu-ally any coin.

Some of the most popular and well-known precious metal rare coins were minted roughly between the 1890s and 1933. These pre-1933 "common date" or "generic" gold and silver coins, as they are typically called, include the gold Liberty Head, Indian Head (see Figure 18.1), and St. Gaudens as well as the Morgan and Peace Silver Dollars.★ But common date rare coins differ from exceptionally rare ones from the same period like the singular gold 1933 Double Eagle—which you would be lucky to buy for under $10 million if you could legally own it—in that the market for them is relatively liquid: There are millions of common date coins, like the St. Gaudens and Liberty Head, on the market, but only a few thousand in great condition.[7] Common date coins are abundant enough that most investors can afford them and thus profit from investing in the rare coin market. With gold trading near $670 an ounce as this was written, a good quality Morgan Silver Dollar could be had for $100 and common date one-ounce gold coins for around $1,000.

Figure 18.1   1932 Indian Head Gold Coin
SOURCE: Austin Rare Coins.

★You can see images of these coins by going to www.pcgs.com and clicking on the Coin Guide tab on the bottom left of the website. You can also Google the coin name and find images on dealers' websites. I generally go to goldinfo.net, which is linked to Austin Rare Coins.

What Is A "Common Date" or "Generic" Coin?

A "common date" or "generic" gold or silver coin is the name given to the millions that were minted in the United States roughly between 1890 and 1933, the year in which the U.S. government prohibited citizens from owning gold bullion and when it stopped minting gold coins. Although several coins from this period are exceptionally rare (like the 1907 "Rolled Edge" $10 Gold Piece, of which less than fifty survive in mint state), common date coins were minted in large quantities and many survive today. A typical generic would be one of the coins listed in Table 18.1, but generally in a grade below MS-65, since the coins are rarer in higher grades, and hence far more expensive—by tens, if not hundreds of thousands of dollars!

A classic common date rare coin is the 1904 Liberty Head $20 Gold Coin, of which over six million coins were minted. However, only a few hundred thousand of them survive today, and of

Table 18.1   A Sample of Common Date Coins in MS-63

Coin	Year	Mintage (m)	Price	Premium over Raw Gold/Silver
$20 Liberty Head	1904	6.3	$1,050	62%
$20 St. Gaudens	1924	4.3	$900	38%
$10 Indian Head	1926	1.0	$1,450	346%
$10 Liberty Head	1899	1.3	$1,250	285%
$5 Indian Head	1909-D	3.4	$2,950	1715%
$5 Liberty Head	1899	1.7	$950	485%
$2.5 Liberty Head	1907	0.3	$1,050	1192%
$2.5 Indian Head	1929	0.5	$1,350	1562%
Morgan Silver Dollar	1883	12.3	$50	285%
Peace Silver Dollar	1925	10.2	$35	169%

All premiums (approximate) are based on gold and silver ounce prices of $650 and $13, respectively. $20 coins contain roughly one ounce, $10 coins half an ounce, $5 coins one-quarter of an ounce and $2.5 coins one-eighth of an ounce of gold. Silver dollars contain roughly an ounce of silver.

SOURCE: R.S.Yeoman, *A Guide Book to United States Coins, 2007* (Atlanta: Whitman Publishing, 2006).

(continued)

those the ones that have been certified make up the coin's population. A coin's population determines its rarity, and evidently rarer coins are worth more. Table 18.1 lists some common dates that have a large population, which makes them less expensive than exceptionally rare coins, but which nevertheless have a fixed amount available. Obvious as it sounds, they will never be minted again, and yet the number of potential buyers will always be rising.

What Is Meant by "Double" Eagle?

When American gold coins began to be minted in the late 18th century, Congress ordered that the first gold coins be called "eagles" with a value of 10 dollars and containing roughly half an ounce of gold. Half-eagles worth $5 and quarter-eagles worth $2.5 also went into circulation, and double-eagles with a value of $20 and containing just under a full ounce of gold were minted for circulation for the first time in 1850. Thus, the list above is ordered from double eagles ($20) at the top to quarter eagles ($2.5) at the bottom.

I believe that many pre-1933 gold and silver rare coins will continue to rise faster than the metal prices themselves in the years to come. In the 1980s, a great number of investors were attracted to the rare coin market—many out of concern about the rising government deficit at the time—and while interest diminished during the '90s stock market boom, investment demand has risen in recent years as gold and silver have continued to climb, while the number of coins remains relatively fixed. (There's always the unlikely chance that more coins can be found somewhere.) Each time gold has rallied, rare coins have risen much faster, as buyers have entered the market to purchase the dwindling supply of coins. If the dollar continues to fall and gold breaks above $1,000 and higher, as I expect, many newcomers to the market—particularly middle class Americans diversifying their assets away from turbulent financial markets—will force a sharp squeeze of the tiny rare coin market, which probably trades less than $500 million in a typical year;[8] that's about the value traded in less than an hour on a slow day at the New York Stock Exchange. And if the dollar truly does collapse, there will be few financial assets in which to take refuge from a fall in global wealth. U.S. government bonds, the traditional asset class to hide in during times of financial turmoil, would likely decline sharply in value. And the very few stores of value that are trusted beyond bonds would skyrocket. Ultimately, there is nothing safer than gold that you can hold in your hand, and coins minted long ago, by the nature of their rarity and accepted value, will be as safe as gold—but far more valuable.

Some basic ideas behind investing profitably in rare coins.

Below are some broad ideas you should keep in mind before investing in rare coins. As with most major purchases, you need to consider both price and quality to arrive at a good investment. The following ideas will help you ascertain both.

1. **Rare coins are not a short term investment and prices can be volatile.** If you are considering investing in rare coins, you must first accept that a rare coin is an investment that you should expect to hold for *at least* two or three years, something that you want to buy and lock away as one of your most valuable possessions. As such, I think rare coins should represent less than 10 percent of your investments. I like to think of an exceptional rare coin as one of my children's college saving funds, a store of wealth that is secure from financial adversity that I know will be available in the future. Profits can come suddenly, but most experts advise against investing for short term profits in the rare coin market, even though there have been several important periods when prices have risen by leaps and bounds. While a sharp fall in the dollar could make rare coins begin to surge in value, profit in rare coins usually goes to those who are patient. If you might need to sell it in a hurry in less than two years, you should think twice about buying a rare coin.

   As is well known in the gold business, the bid-ask spread in the rare coins market is large. What this effectively means is that a rare coin shop generally needs to raise its coin prices at least 15 percent above cost, and that it will buy coins back at a discount. This is a low volume business of high-value products, and like other businesses of this kind—like luxury goods stores—the margins have to be high for the firms to be profitable. As a result, when you buy a rare coin you are generally starting out under water: you need the coin you bought to rise by 15 percent or more just to break even. This is why it is best to wait some time before selling. Although rare coins have outperformed stocks over time, some investors steer clear of the market, or risk trying to buy wisely on eBay or in some other direct market where there are no guarantees, because the large mark-ups at coin shops bother them. I think getting the right price is important, but so is buying from a reputable firm. Anyone entering the rare coins market should consider both carefully.

2. **Always beware of rip-off coin shops and websites.** Keep in mind what I have said throughout this part of the book: gold has a way of attracting swindlers who will try to take advantage of you. A Saint Gaudens gold coin minted over 80 years ago may seem priceless, but millions of them were minted. Although a far lower number survive in truly superb condition, many are less rare than you would think. *Understand what you are buying before you write a check.* Even if you are buying from a dealer or website that you trust, as with any gold or silver bullion or rare coin price, compare the price with others you find on the Internet. If a dealer or website is selling a coin that is 40 percent over- or underpriced, something is not right!

3. **Pick coins that are popular with both investors and collectors.** Many rare coins, like pennies and nickels, have been great investments. And if you decided to pick up Bowers' *The Expert's Guide to Collecting & Investing in Rare Coins*, a 600-pager, or the hundreds of other books published on the subject, with a great deal of time and effort you might discover a way to profit from 1905 music box tokens. But you might also find that these century-old tokens can still be had for a few dollars because hardly anybody knows they exist![9] And perhaps most importantly: Hardly anybody cares. One of the most important things to keep in mind when buying a rare gold or silver coin for investment is that you will want to sell it in the future: Stick with precious metal coins that are widely desirable, that any coin dealer is familiar with, and you will find that there are really only a handful of rare coins that are truly and ultimately liquid. There will generally be a buyer for them when you need to sell.

Keep in mind that many extremely rare coins are inexpensive. They only become expensive when many people want to buy them. And there are other special, widely recognized coins that some collectors have been waiting for years to get their hands on and would be willing to pay a high price for. Unless you want to invest the lengthy time and deep effort needed to become a serious coin collector/investor, I recommend staying with pre-1933 common date gold Liberty Heads, Indian Heads, and St. Gaudens gold and Peace and Morgan Silver Dollar coins that have been on collectors and investors' minds for decades. These are rare in that there is a fixed supply of them on the market, and yet common enough that any dealer is very familiar with them. (Several of them are listed in the section entitled What Is A "Common Date" or "Generic" Coin?)

4. **Only buy certified rare coins.** Here is an opportunity to lose a lot of money: buy a rare coin that has not been certified. (See Figure 18.2 to see what a certified rare coin looks like.) Unless the price of a rare coin is very near the price of gold (say a premium below 15 percent, as is the case with the very common pre-1933 Swiss Helvetia) its premium over gold will be based on the coin's authenticity, grade and rarity. Huge premiums, which can run into the millions of dollars, are paid for rare coins of exceptional rarity and condition. For example, the 1870-S Three-Dollar Gold Piece in good condition, which contains less than an ounce of gold, is worth perhaps three million dollars! With certification, a coin's authenticity and graded condition are clearly established so that both buyer and seller have only price to debate on.★ Though price is market determined—and one must do a little research on the Internet to determine what the right one is— you can cover the other variables in a coin's value by limiting your investments to certified rare coins.

There are a great many subtleties in coin grading about which hundreds of books have been written, but basically coins are graded on a scale of 1 to 70: a coin graded 70 is flawless, as if fresh from the

---

★Very occasionally, someone, usually an expert, will find a coin that appears to have been graded too low. Taking a chance, he or she might break the seal of the clear plastic case containing the coin and send the raw coin to be certified with the hope that a new grade will be higher.

mint, and 1s are reserved for coins with virtually unrecognizable images and words. Coins graded between 60 and 70, representing their good condition, are regarded as being "uncirculated" and in "mint state." So a 1913-D St. Gaudens coin, with a "-D" indicating it was minted in Denver (see Table 18.2), in very good condition might have a grade of MS-65. But a dealer might call it a "Saint in 65," as the "MS" is redundant: anything above a 60 will be in mint state.

Although there are others, the Professional Coin Grading Service (PCGS) and the Numismatic Guaranty Corporation (NGC) are the two most respected coin grading companies in the United States. Each coin they receive for grading is subject to examination by numismatic experts in a rigid certification process in which the final product is an authenticated and graded coin, such as the one shown in Figure 18.2. Each certified coin is sonically sealed in a tamper-evident clear plastic holder that displays its biographical information, the firm's trademark hologram, a bar code, and a unique number that registers the coin with either PCGS or NGC. You can find greater detail about the grading process at their respective websites.

5. **When investing, buy high quality rare coins.** Here's the simple reason why you generally want to buy pre-1933 coins (again, referring specifically to that deep market of coins minted roughly during the 40 years ending in 1933) with a high grade: graded below MS-60, coins like gold St. Gaudens and Morgan Silver Dollars with scratches and other defects are so common that they trade near the value of their

Table 18.2   Mints and Mintmarks

Mintmarks are letters found on coins that show where they were minted. You will find them on many of the coins in your pockets on the "heads" side.

C	Charlotte, North Carolina (gold coins only; 1838–1861)
CC	Carson City, Nevada (1870–1893)
D	Dahlonega, Georgia (gold coins only; 1838–1861)
D	Denver, Colorado (1906 to date)
O	New Orleans, Louisiana (1838–1861; 1879–1909)
P	Philadelphia, Pennsylvania (1793 to date; P absent in early years)
S	San Francisco, California (1854 to date)
W	West Point New York (1984 to date)

As you might expect, some of the most valuable rare coins were minted in Carson City, Charlotte and Dahlonega, where coin production ended more than a century ago.

SOURCE: R.S. Yeoman, *A Guide Book to United States Coins, 2007* (Atlanta: Whitman Publishing, 2006).

Figure 18.2   Example of a Certified Rare Coin
SOURCE: Austin Rare Coins.

metallic content. Actually, the coins are so common that they are rarely even graded, since grading costs around $20 a coin, hence reducing potential profit. If gold is trading at $650 an ounce, you can probably find an 80-year-old gold ounce coin in poor condition not too far above that price. But unless you just want it for a collection, this would probably be a bad *investment* because such a coin would be unlikely to outperform gold or silver bullion prices. And, perhaps more importantly, it would be far easier to sell a modern bullion coin, so—aesthetics aside—why even buy a scratched up St. Gaudens when you can get a pristine 2008 American Eagle gold coin straight from the U.S. Mint?

6. **Find a dealer you can trust and verify that you are getting good prices.** If you are planning to make a major investment in rare coins, I would strongly recommend that you take your time in finding a good rare coin dealer, as discussed in chapter 16. In addition to having a verifiably solid reputation established over at least a decade, a good dealer will listen to what you are looking for—for instance, "I want to make a bold bet to profit from rising gold prices" or "I just want protection"—and suggest diverse investment strategies at a competitive price. If some coins are suggested that you are not familiar with, remember that it is best—at least until you learn more about rare coins—to stick with well-known coins that are highly liquid. You might already have a few coins in mind and he or she might suggest others. But when it comes down to settling on prices, keep in mind that you should check them with competitors and at websites like www.pcgs.com. Prices will rarely be exactly the same, but at least you will get a sense of the kind of deal you are getting. This could take some time, but you will find that prices can vary widely. As discussed chapter 16, you will need to find a balance between price and value of service. A trustworthy dealer could cost a little more, but the relationship might be worth the price.

7. **If you are looking for high-end rare coins, consult with an expert.** In this chapter I have been referring to modestly priced gold rare coins that are not worth more than, say, 15 times the value of their metallic content. (See What Is a "Common Date" or "Generic Coin?") But some of the biggest investment gains have been in rare coins of which only a handful are available, such as the "common date" coins discussed above that are in uncommon condition. Here's an example: A 1909-D Saint Gaudens $20 gold coin in MS-60 was worth about $1,800 when these words were written, but the same coin in MS-67—a much better preserved coin of greater rarity—was valued at a whopping $175,000.

But such a coin would generally be traded between coin experts acting on behalf of clients that pay them a fee, or perhaps a mark-up on the coin's cost, to execute the transaction. Many high-end coin investors ask that coin shops actively seek specific unique coins that might take an expert years to locate. Others are simply looking for any special opportunity to acquire truly rare coins that can cost more than a new car—or fleet. Quite often, coin buyers prefer to remain anonymous, as was the case in the 2002 auction of a 1933 gold Double Eagle. The opening bid was $2.5 million, but few know who wrote the 7.6-million-dollar check after the Sotheby's gavel was finally slammed. The high-end rare coin club is exclusive, but there are quite a few gems selling in the $10,000 to $30,000 price range for those looking to make more modest acquisitions.

While an amateur could distinguish between a coin graded in MS-60 and another in MS-67, given the evident visual dissimilarity, the subtle differences between a 66 and 67—or the actual numeric grade assigned to any unique coin—can only be determined with precision by an expert. If you are considering investing in unique rare coins running into many thousands of dollars in value, you should spend some time finding a trustworthy professional individual or company with a great reputation. This is the only way to ensure a given coin's authenticity and grade, and trust is vital when it comes to determining value. Because, although you can try to check prices online, the rarer coins become, the less pricing information is available. And quite often, the last price seen for a given ultra-rare coin could have been set at a trade made years in the past, making its present value more difficult to ascertain. The coins in Table 18.3, which include some of the rarest in the world, only trade every few years. And the top two may never change hands again. (See Table 18.3)

Some Final Thoughts on Investing in Rare Coins

A perennial rule of thumb has been to invest in the highest grade coin that one can afford. And judging by the price performance of the extraordinary coins in Table 18.3, it is clear that the rarest of the rare have appreciated the most in the last 25 years. Ultra-rare coins were rising by leaps and bounds even as gold and silver prices sagged in the 1980s and '90s. But this pattern doesn't necessarily have to continue in the future. Perhaps after the extraordinary rise in coins worth, say, $50,000 or more, these will begin to rise more slowly than some of the lower-valued, more common coins that have been left behind—the ones more closely tied to the market price of gold and silver.

Table 18.3 A Sample of Exceptionally Rare Coins

Year	Coin	Grade	Metal	Value		Gain	
				1980	2007	Total	per year
1907	Indian Head Double Eagle Pattern	Gem Proof	gold	$500,000	$12,500,000	2,400%	12.7%
1933	St. Gaudens Double Eagle★	Uncirculated	gold	$250,000	$8,500,000	3,300%	14.0%
1804	Bust Silver Dollar	Choice Proof	silver	$250,000	$5,000,000	1,900%	11.7%
1894-S	Barber Dime	Proof	silver	$100,000	$1,500,000	1,400%	10.6%
1913	Liberty Nickel	Choice Proof	nickel	$250,000	$6,000,000	2,300%	12.5%
1822	Half Eagle	Extremely Fine	gold	$650,000	$5,000,000	669%	7.8%
1792	Half Disme	Very Fine	silver	$5,000	$85,000	1,600%	11.1%
1794	Silver Dollar	Extremely Fine	silver	$25,000	$250,000	900%	8.9%
1796	Quarter Dollar	Extremely Fine	silver	$7,500	$40,000	433%	6.4%
1895	Silver Dollar	Choice Proof	silver	$17,500	$45,000	157%	3.6%

★Although there is a case in court relating to the legal ownership of 10 1933 Double Eagles, as of this writing, ownership by private citizens is illegal, except for one example. (See Paul Gilkes, "Government Denies 1933 $20 Claims," *Coin World*, Sept. 3, 2007.)

SOURCE: Jeff Garett, author (with Ron Guth) of *100 Greatest U.S. Coins, 2nd Edition* (Atlanta: Whitman Publishing, 2005).

That the surge in high-end coin values has coincided with the extreme rise in incomes among the top one percent of the U.S. population should not be surprising. Over the last two decades, millionaires and billionaires have clearly moved part of their enormous wealth into rare coins, and naturally they have tended to acquire the best of the best, and the price of gold or silver was probably far from their minds at the time. (If you were buying a two-million-dollar gold coin, would you care if an ounce of gold were worth $800 or $2,000?) But most others, who could only aspire to rare coins that were closer to their metallic value, were clearly very sensitive to changes in gold and silver prices and perhaps stayed away from the rare coin market because metal prices were weak. Hence more common rare coins lagged the rarest.

But a more likely reason was simply that nobody cared about investing in coins at the time. During the 1990s the investment world was focused on the stock market and gold probably never even crossed most people's minds. Who cared if gold was up or down 3 percent if many stocks were doubling in value? Gold and silver prices were being monitored by the handful of people that were worried far too soon, as it turned out, about issues like American debt that have only recently erupted into the serious economic problems—and growing financial risks—that we are beginning to face today. Now that financial markets and the dollar could begin to break down, as many are expecting today, I think the value of a broad array of rare coins, including the most common and moderately-priced, could begin to rise sharply—and faster than gold and silver.

While there are more than a million active American coin collectors, rare coin investors are very small in number—certainly far less than 1 percent of the number of stock market investors. But if gold were to break $1,000 and silver $17 an ounce as stocks and bond markets became mine fields, as they were in the 1970s, a growing number of middle class men and women would likely turn to the rare coin market seeking to protect their wealth thanks mostly to the Internet. Both the Wall Street executive and the Kansan farmer, who could never—and probably *would* never—walk into a coin shop, can now surf the Web to find gold and silver easily. And in time, if precious metals continue to climb in value, many people will learn that rare coin prices tend to rise faster than the metals of which they are made.

Gold and silver coins have only been selling on the Internet for a little over ten years, many of them bad years for precious metals prices, like the 1990s, when E-Trade was a far more popular investment site. Although it has yet to happen, tens of millions of dollars in coin orders—a tiny investment speck in the trillion dollar financial world—could conceivably be placed on precious metals websites in a single night. And it remains to be seen how a sudden rush of capital into rare coins would affect the miniscule market as firms scrambled to fill orders. Precious metals websites, which after all have only been operating for a handful of years, have yet to handle a massive sudden flow of orders. Although there have been flurries of intense activity during disasters like 9/11 and Y2K, these have been short-lived mostly because central banks successfully contained the price of gold and prevented financial panic, as they have done many times in the past. But if gold began to surge out of central banks' control, as I believe will eventually happen, there would naturally be an intense flow of orders into gold shops.

Picture the few dozen poorly-staffed coin shops across the country, which handle an extremely low number of orders each day. Aside from Internet orders, I believe a typical precious metals specialist at any major firm is lucky to have more than ten phone orders in a day, and there are probably less than 2,000 such specialists across the country. It is a tiny business. When a metals specialist gets an order for, say, 10 Saint Gaudens double eagles in MS-64, his or her firm rarely holds them in inventory: The firm must go out in the market and buy them, hoping that the price is low and that other firms are not out in the market looking for the same coins. Unfortunately for them, when rising gold prices cause the common date market to heat up, demand spikes and supply dries up: coin holders, unsure if they will be selling too cheaply, invariably decide to sell only to high bidders, which causes a chain reaction of rising prices. This is why in early 2006, when gold rose over 25 percent, several popular common date coins rose by double that percentage.

Buying rare coins used to mean going to a coin shop that could generally be found only in cities and large towns, a fact that made the market all but inaccessible to many people. One had to leave the house. At shops, buyers saw only the inventory each establishment had on hand, or could order unseen coins from the dealer or magazines at the risk of obtaining a coin of lesser quality than expected. Although many coins they could see were graded, these grades reflected the opinion of an individual shop owner and not an independent specialist. And some sellers were no doubt tempted to grade a newly purchased $10 Indian Head in MS-62 as a more valuable MS-63.

Today, the Internet has made the rare coin market far more transparent and the ease of buying and selling is greater than ever. Furthermore, with PCGS and NGC grading, any coin can be certified with an opinion widely accepted among investors and collectors, which facilitates the confident participation of novices in the market. Prices can be compared among a great many firms online, and the openness of the Internet itself tends to reveal unethical firms quickly. Considering these factors, the rare coin market today is truly a relatively new way to preserve part of one's wealth and diversify assets away from other financial markets. I think this tiny little market, a speck in the $140 trillion global asset ocean, could be a mini-NASDAQ in the making.

Chapter 19

Why Silver Might Rise More Than Gold

Although this book recommends buying gold, the reader may have noticed that in the preceding chapter dealing with rare coins I often mentioned silver. I did so partly because many rare coins are worth substantially more than their metallic content, and hence the market price of both gold and silver have a lesser effect on the value of many rare coins made of the metals. (This explains why some rare coins rose in value after 1980, while gold and silver declined.) But I also suggested silver coins alongside gold ones because I think this poor man's gold could rise as much, or perhaps more sharply than gold in the years ahead. (See Figure 19.1.)

In a free market, it is axiomatic that the price of any asset will rise when demand increases above supply. The argument I've made for gold, at its core, is that investment demand will rise sharply as supply remains constrained in the years ahead. But while gold holds the precious metals spotlight, silver demand has been substantially higher than what mining companies have produced for many years. As with gold, when governments eventually decide

Figure 19.1   Price of an Ounce of Silver
SOURCE: Bloomberg.

or are forced to reduce the silver they have been dumping on the markets for decades—since they are generally not replenishing supplies—both silver and gold should begin to rise sharply. This supply shortfall in the future has been discussed extensively by gold experts, but few have argued that it would be smart to buy silver, a sometimes highly volatile precious metal/commodity that can rise or fall 10 percent in a single day.

Perhaps some investors fearfully remember the bubble of 1980, when the Hunt family of Texas and the House of Saud tried to corner the relatively small silver market with disastrous results: silver briefly skyrocketed to $50 an ounce, then collapsed when the plot was uncovered and the Hunts alone lost almost two billion dollars.[1] The price of silver plunged 50 percent on a single day, Silver Thursday, March 27, 1980. A different fate was met by Warren Buffett, perhaps the most successful stock market investor in history, who bought 130 million ounces in 1997 below $5 an ounce and made a healthy profit when he sold years later. But the short term flurry of buying his move provoked has not helped silver rise to become an asset that many pay attention to. Try to get a book on silver investing and you will come across only a handful, and beyond the information provided by The Silver Institute or GFMS, it is hard to find reliable data and analysis on the metal outside the institute's website or Internet sites like Silver-Investor.com that the small number of silver aficionados go to.

As with gold, silver supply comes from the mining industry (71 percent of total supply), scrap selling (21 percent) and government sales (8 percent).[2] But there are two important factors that have a significant effect on silver's supply that are absent with gold. First, most of the silver mined each year is used up in industrial processes: although part is recovered as scrap and recycled, most of what has been mined in the last one hundred years is simply gone forever. This is not the case with gold, as most of the gold mined and refined over thousands of years exists today.

A second important factor that will constrain future supply is that, while the U.S. government holds substantial gold, it has finally sold all its silver. In 1970, our government owned 375 million ounces of silver, what was left of the U.S. silver purchase program initiated in 1933 to help the depressed mining industry of that time.[3] Today we own zero, and to supply the U.S. Mint with the silver needed to mint the great number of silver coins sold each year, the government needs to buy silver on the open market. Silver sales by other countries are now necessary to prevent prices from climbing sharply to the detriment of the many companies that use silver as an industrial input. But the existing above ground stocks of silver have been depleted severely in the last 15 years to meet the mining deficit and China and India, two of the largest holders today, are believed to be near the bottom of their supplies. Now that the U.S. has depleted its silver stockpile and other governments have been reducing theirs, as well, silver expert David Morgan believes there are roughly 500 million ounces of silver bullion available for investment, which is about a quarter of the 2 billion ounces of gold that are believed to exist in bullion form.[4] And silver continues to be consumed—permanently—by industry.

Of the 912 million ounces of silver produced last year, roughly half of it, about 430 million ounces, was used in industrial applications. Another 145 million was used in photographic processes, which is down by about a third from what was being used ten years ago.[5] Those expecting the advent of the digital camera to crush the price of silver, a vital input in old school photography, would be surprised to learn that only 16 percent of all silver demand today is used in photography. The remaining demand is from producers of jewelry, silverware and coins and medals, as well as a completely new source: silver exchange traded funds. Trading under the ticker "SLV" since 2006, the iShares Silver Trust held 141 million ounces of silver as of the writing of this book. As with gold ETFs, investors can now purchase silver without needing to store it, and can trade in and out of silver positions at ease with the click of a mouse.

The price of silver is highly correlated with that of gold: The metals tend to move in the same direction. However, you should always keep in mind that silver is far more volatile than gold, and is hence not for the light-hearted. It can rise faster than gold, or drop a sharp 9 percent in a day while gold falls 2 percent. That being said, even if we avoid a dollar crisis, I think silver prices will continue to rise driven by falling government supply, strong demand driven in part by ETF investors, and the continual depletion of existing inventories that cannot be recovered. Morgan estimates that 1.5 billion ounces of silver were used up between 1990 and 2005.[6] On the other hand, if the United States is going into a recession, industrial demand for silver could falter, leading the price down if investment demand is not sufficient to make up for it. And if central banks become more concerned about the fate of the dollar, they would buy gold before silver. I am optimistic about silver, but keep these factors in mind before buying.

Conclusion

Don't Be A Gold Bug: Sell When It Is Time To Sell

The late economist John Kenneth Galbraith coined the term "conventional wisdom" to describe ideas that most people find acceptable and true, even if the concepts themselves are not.[1] Lab workers seek scientifically-provable verities, but public relations experts concerned with audience reactions focus on and design concepts that are agreeable and convenient to most, easy to understand and promise to prevent awkwardness and dislocation of life.[2] The conventional wisdom, Galbraith said, deals less with the world as it is and more with the way most people see it. Hence a politician who, concerned about mounting federal liabilities, calls for citizens to pay higher taxes and accept lower government benefits is unelectable today. These sacrifices, necessary as they will be in the not distant future, are incompatible with what attracts millions of voters to each of the nation's two dominant political parties: Republicans and Democrats are elected largely on the promise that their constituencies will be protected from government-inflicted economic pain.

191

Eighty years ago, when the dollar was literally worth gold, politicians and the public thought in completely different terms. The conventional wisdom held a balanced federal budget as sacrosanct, the very economic foundation of the country, as Galbraith pointed out. President Franklin D. Roosevelt—not long before changing his mind—said in his first inaugural address in 1932: "Revenue must cover expenditures by one means or another. Any government, like any family, can for a year spend a little more than it earns. But you and I know that a continuation of that habit means the poorhouse." Yet the historical axiom that government and family books need to balance, intuitively appealing as it is, was not debunked by sophisticated new ideas, but rather by the dire circumstances of the Great Depression. It was the brutality of and inability to escape an economic collapse never experienced before that forced leaders to think the unthinkable and consider long-shunned economic ideas. In time it became acceptable for the government to spend more than it received, at least during economic downturns; and in the years ahead, always.

Watching CNBC each morning over breakfast before going into work, I am accustomed to hearing bits of our generation's economic conventional wisdom expressed by the world's financial experts. The bulging federal debt and continuing deficits are not news—after all, most of us have always lived under them—and the focus in today's economic slowdown, or perhaps soon-to-be recession, is on the Federal Reserve. *How deeply will it cut interest rates to contain the credit crisis and get the real estate market back on its feet?* we ask, most of us believing that the Fed preserves the power to reestablish financial order simply by encouraging further borrowing through lower interest rates. The nation's balance sheet—by which I mean that of the government and consumers—is stretched like never before, and yet the conventional wisdom continues to hold that more rate cuts will once again make things right.

But the September 18, 2007, Federal Reserve reduction in the Fed Funds rate by half a percentage point made clear the new challenges its chairman, Ben Bernanke faces in an effort to soothe financial markets and strengthen the economy. Because, unlike his predecessor, who never had to worry much about the strength of the dollar, Bernanke's first rate cut caused a sharp decline in the greenback that day as well as the following week and month, and gold rallied strongly. All other major economies had no reason to reduce rates at the time, and some were still expected to raise them, so there was even less demand for the lower-yielding dollar, which had already been declining for several years. Cutting interest rates, which generally leads to a higher amount of dollars in circulation, forced the world's central banks to absorb even more dollar reserves than their bloated physical and digital vaults already hold, buying up the currency that private investors continue to sell in an effort to maintain exchange rate balance.

The pressure is greatest on China, which is rapidly emerging as the world's biggest dollar hoarder—and our most important creditor—in its uneasy effort to maintain a weak currency, the indispensable driver of its export-led economy. The country has been struggling in recent years to contain runaway liquidity, which has been prompted, to a large degree, by its need to buy hundreds of billions of dollars in the market each year. But propping up the dollar was easier when American interest rates were climbing, which made the greenback relatively more attractive; now that the Fed is cutting rates, which weakens our currency, China will need to buy dollars at a faster rate than before and hence inject *even more* liquidity into its economy. The country faces the prospect of surging inflation and, hoping to contain it, the government ordered a freeze on all government prices, like oil, electricity and water in September 2007.[3] But these measures do little to contain asset bubbles emerging in home prices and the stock market, which today trades at earnings multiples approaching those of the pre-collapse U.S. stock market of 2000.

In addition to the intensifying monetary pressure being applied by the Fed on China through rate cuts, our political leaders are also raising the heat on our vital lender. "I really do believe we are at an inflection point," U.S. Treasury Secretary Henry Paulson said on September 10, 2007. Speaking with concern about bills being pushed through the U.S. Senate intended to punish China economically, he made a stern warning: "When we look at taking unilateral actions aimed at another nation, this can have enormous repercussions to our economic well-being . . . We are playing with fire."[4] Perhaps to appease Chinese leaders, who are being criticized internally for using funds to accumulate American liabilities and dollar reserves that could be used for other purposes, in just a year Paulson has traveled four times to China, making evident the country's rapidly magnifying importance in the global financial system. I think a far more important question than *What will the Fed do?* is *What would happen if China is finally forced to let the dollar fall?*

Still, financial eyes remain fixated on the Fed's next move, and its effect on *our* economy. But the center of economic gravity has been shifting away from Bernanke's office and toward the other side of the world. Unconcerned for decades about the value of our currency, the conventional wisdom in the United States has long been that it is the rest of the world's problem: To keep us buying their products, other countries need to continue subsidizing our purchases by indirectly lending us the bulk of their net savings. And these nations have followed the Japanese model that has been so beneficial to the U.S.—China, Russia, Brazil, India, and many other countries have not collected on U.S. debts or cashed in paper U.S. currency, making their accumulating dollar reserves as useful to them as Monopoly money, colorful paper that cannot be exchanged for real goods. Our liabilities just pile up in foreign vaults, at an intensifying pace.

As the greenback continues to fall, a number of economists have warned that the mounting international imbalances in the dollar-based monetary system, which since 1971 is no longer based on gold, could end in a catastrophe. "Let us be blunt about it," warned economist Martin Wolf in the *Financial Times* in 2004. "The U.S. is on the comfortable path to ruin. It is being driven along a road of ever rising deficits and debt, both external and fiscal, that risk destroying the country's credit and the global role of its currency."[5] But the sanguine conventional wisdom that Bretton Woods II can endure will not end because of stark warnings, such as Wolf's; after all, the heads of a great many international financial organizations, like the International Monetary Fund and Bank of International Settlements, as well as Paul Volker, perhaps the world's most respected central banker, have openly expressed deep concern about the financial paradigm the world lives under. But, as Galbraith said, the world's conventional wisdom is never brought down by ideas, but rather the march of events.

And what events could these be? This book has discussed factors pointing to a deep economic slowdown driven by our mounting debt, which has originated in real estate, the most important American asset. As the Fed begins a new cycle of interest rate cuts likely resulting in further dollar depreciation, the world's central banks will do their best to maintain exchange rate stability effectively by printing money to buy our money—and they can only hope the world doesn't start openly questioning the value of paper money being created at increasing speed. But if we begin to consume less of other countries' products because of a debt-driven recession—which, as pointed out in Chapter 10, most Americans polled are expecting—what need will these nations have to continue propping up the dollar? When I began writing this book in early 2007, economists worried that housing prices might not rise for a year or two. In late September, several TRS portfolio managers, analysts and I met with a major Wall Street firm's financial research team, which surprised us by openly anticipating a 13 to 15 percentage price fall in the median American home value, the first brutal decline since the Great Depression. As of writing these lines, the National Association of Realtors had reduced its home sales forecast for the ninth time in 2007, and indicated the housing market downswing was worsening.[6]

Though I have yet to read or hear it, I think in time someone will predict that we may face a protracted deep recession in the years ahead. Though it would be hard to make the case for such a terrible prediction today, it is certainly true that the liabilities accumulated in the American economy are stunning—more so than ever—and excessive debt is what depressions are made of. The fantastic rise in wealth during the last decade was driven in large part by mountains of credit, less so by American income, and the national saving rate will have to climb, if not now, then later, to the detriment of our economic growth. The larger homes, the better cars and the many other things have been purchased by borrowing from the future, a future that we, as Americans, have always viewed optimistically. We have been encouraged to do so. But most economists understand that our savings rate must be restored. Changing the savings rate label and saying repeatedly that we are wealthier than ever will not change the fact that we rely on the world's savings to fund our consumption.

And yet we will soon be facing this paradox of thrift at a time when a large portion of the population will be retiring, drawing on accumulated wealth by selling stocks, bonds and homes to a younger population that collectively has substantially less than its elders in the bank with which to purchase them. The required surge in benefit payments to the senior population will almost inevitably raise the budget deficit, eventually forcing the government to raise taxes or reduce benefits, actions that likely would depress economic activity further. To address this 65-trillion-dollar wind blowing from the nation's future, perhaps the draconian solution of simply ignoring a large part of the government's obligations to millions of retirees, a possibility that has tacitly been raised in some newspapers, could mitigate effects of the debt problem. But who would bet on legislators committing collective political suicide? Great national sacrifices no doubt will be required not long from now.

An increase in American savings would be deflationary, since prices would fall due to the consequent decline in demand for products and services. But the prospect of deflation, such as Japan faced not long ago, would be met head-on by Fed Chairman Ben Bernanke, a Great Depression scholar. He understands the dangers of contracting prices—like the ones we face in the real estate market today—and has made clear his willingness to employ unconventional measures to create inflation. Leaving aside the potentially adverse implications of even greater Fed involvement in the economy (in new and potentially destabilizing ways), yet another dramatic reflationary injection of monetary stimulus—such as the last one applied under Alan Greenspan, the deepest in U. S. history—might be the final catalyst for the dollar to crash. But in one way or another, a great many new dollars are likely to be printed: Inflation will be made to arrive. Bernanke has made so much very clear. Paul Volker, by giving credibility and value to the dollar via the draconian monetary medicine of high interest rates, drove down the value of gold in 1980. His descendant today, who stands ready to print money, is likely to become gold's friend.

But the world is already awash with dollars. Buying trillions more of them—and perhaps allowing our debt to rise above 400 percent of our GDP—to maintain currency competitiveness would likely force a country like China to create double-digit inflation in its economy, a risk it would be unlikely to take. Eventually, I don't see how the world will avoid throwing in the towel on the dollar and allowing it to fall sharply. I think our liabilities are simply too large to sustain the present exchange rate as the economy slows, and yet a sharp fall in the dollar would cause a great many other problems that are difficult to visualize, particularly considering the gargantuan size of the derivatives market and the slimly capitalized banking system, still with a balance sheet geared for the good times. "Too big to fail" is a term that has been applied to save a company or two. What would happen if financial collapse arrived by the dozen?

Having lived through two devaluations, during which collapse simply arrived following years in which most economists largely ignored mounting imbalances, I have spent a great deal of time trying to learn about investing in precious metals because I think the odds of a dollar collapse—meaning a collapse of the world's monetary foundation—are high.

If the dollar crashed, an event almost incomprehensible in its dire effects, I believe it would be difficult for the euro, perhaps expected to become the new currency anchor of the world in time, surviving in its present form. The latent national differences, which lay dormant in present calm economic times, would likely surface with intensity under monetary strain. The region's exporting nations, like France and Italy, would likely clamor for devaluation, while Spain and Ireland, beneficiaries of a strong euro, would fight for the opposite.

Consider Italy, whose export economy has already suffered more than most European nations due to the falling dollar. Unlike California, which cannot secede from the United States, what could ultimately prevent a determined Italy from dumping the nine-year-old euro to regain control of its monetary destiny, which today is decided in Germany under orders spoken in French? To the financial penalties due as a result of tearing up a supposedly unbreakable European treaty, a rising Italian leader, riding triumphantly on an anti-euro populist platform, would simply say, *Send me the bill. We are recovering our monetary sovereignty with the lira!* With Italy gone, the euro would be crippled and other countries would likely also abandon it in time, but well behind the foreign exchange traders that would already be dumping it en masse. But what would they buy?

Gold is the only widely accepted monetary asset that cannot be printed. A politician cannot claim it is strong or weak; it is what it is—a finite store of value that for centuries served as the basis for determining the value of all things. When paper money was redeemable into a fixed amount of gold many years ago, there was a tangible way to know what money was actually worth. Long abandoned as the foundation of the global financial system, now that the dollar's weaknesses are evident to all, perhaps once again the powers that be will be dragged back, kicking and screaming, to gold; into adopting a sound monetary system, one backed to some degree by a precious metal or something else that cannot be printed ad infinitum, as the dollar and countless other currencies have been in recent history. But that will be for world authorities to decide as they grapple with the complex decisions of the future.

Difficult as it is to forecast the future of finance, I think there are years ahead in which gold and silver will rise very sharply against paper currencies. The price of gold, a reflection of the value of tangible and scarce goods, has fallen behind the perceived value of essentially virtual things with unlimited supply, paper currency notes. A brutal adjustment is in sight. If gold rises to $10,000 an ounce, which I believe is probable, this would reflect less a speculative surge in the value of a precious metal present in our civilization for thousands of years, but rather the collapse, once again, of the value of paper money and the consequent rise of inflation. And like stocks and bonds in periods of financial euphoria, gold and silver can overshoot, rise far more than anticipated. But I think in time, once monetary balance is restored, gold and silver will stop being investments promising strong returns and go back to being essentially refined and shaped rocks, as they should be. At that time, stocks should regain their position as the investment of choice and I hope to be selling much of my gold and silver, and I would suggest you do, too.

Notes

Introduction

1. Barry Eichengreen, *Globalizing Capital: A History of the International Monetary System* (Princeton, NJ: Princeton University Press, 1996), 116.

2. The U.S. Treasury reported total international reserves of $70 billion in the fall of 2007, a level Mexico passed more than a year ago. However, U.S. gold reserves are still quite high, as discussed later in the book. If these were included in the calculation and revalued to present market prices, total U.S. reserves would be higher than Mexico's, though still well below those of Japan and China. The point is regarding foreign currency reserves. The U.S. is the only leading economy whose international reserves have been falling in this decade, while those of all others have been rising. The global savings rate cited is after investment.

3. The last debt-to-GDP peak was reached in 1935, when total debt in the United States reached 270 percent of GDP. The 1935 figure is from Bill Gross, "Investment Outlook: The Last Vigilante" Pimco Report, February 2004, www.pimco .com. Historical total debt amounts were taken from the Federal Reserve's Flow of Funds Accounts of the United States, and do not include unfunded liabilities of the federal government, the present value of which would cause the total amounts in the late 2000s to double. GDP is provided by the Bureau of Economic Analysis. Between 1930 and 1933, 8,812 banks suspended operations and less than a third ever reopened. Helen Burns, *The American Banking Community and New Deal Banking Reforms, 1933–1935* (London: Greenwood Press, 1974), 6.

4. The statistic on the amount of U.S. currency circulating outside the United States is from "The Use and Counterfeiting of United States Currency Abroad," Department of the U.S. Treasury, Sept. 2006. Johns Hopkins University Professor Steve Hanke provided me with this useful source.

5. The statistic on the amount of gold sold by central banks is from GFMS, *Gold Survey 2007*.

6. Ibid.

7. Roger Lowenstein, *Buffett: The Making of An American Capitalist* (New York: Random House, 1995), 114–5.

Chapter 1: The $65 Trillion Wind Blowing from Our Future

1. David Walker, Letter to the President, the President of the Senate, and the Speaker of the House of Representatives, December 14, 2005, http://www .gao.gov/financial/fy2005/05gao1.pdf.

2. Linda Bilmes and Joseph Stiglitz, "The Economic Costs of the Iraq War: An Appraisal Three Years After the Beginning of the Conflict," NBER Working Paper No. 12054, Feb. 2006.

3. Walsh Campion, "Facing Debt Limit, U.S. Taps G-Fund," *Wall Street Journal*, 2006.

4. Brian Faler and Alison Fitzgerald, "Congress Raises Debt Cap, Fourth Increase Under Bush," *Bloomberg*, 2006.

5. Jagadeesh Gokhale and Kent Smetters, "Do the Markets Care About the $2.4 Trillion U.S. Deficit?" *Financial Analysts Journal*, March/April 2007.

6. Krishna Guha et al, "Bernanke Warns U.S. of 'Fiscal Crisis'," *Financial Times*, Feb. 2, 2007.

7. One can wonder, as some experts on the subject do, if the deficit is actually falling. "[T]he size of a nation's official debt is purely a function of how the government labels its receipts and payments—what words it uses to describe the monies it takes in and pays out. With one set of words, the country will report one size deficit. With another, it will report a different size deficit. Indeed, with the proper choice of words, governments can make their deficits as large—or as small—as they'd like." Lawrence Kotlikoff and Scott Burns, *The Coming Generational Storm: What You Need to Know About America's Economic Future* (Boston: MIT Press, 2004), xvi.

8. Lawrence Kotlikoff, "Is the United States Bankrupt?" Federal Reserve Bank of St. Louis, Jul/Aug 2006.

9. Gokhale and Smetters, "Do the Markets Care About the $2.4 Trillion U.S. Deficit?"

10. Kotlikoff, "Is the United States Bankrupt?"

11. Guha et al, "Bernanke Warns U.S. of 'Fiscal Crisis'."

12. Kotlikoff and Burns, *The Coming Generational Storm*, xv.

13. Ibid.

14. Ibid.

15. "The Entitlement Panic," *Wall Street Journal*, Aug. 22, 2006.

16. Guha et al, "Bernanke Warns U.S. of 'Fiscal Crisis'."

17. Edmund Andrews. "Brighter '06 Deficit Outlook, But Long Term Looks Grim." *New York Times*, Aug. 18, 2006.

Chapter 2: How Can Families Really Be Getting Richer by Borrowing More?

1. Flow of Funds Accounts of the United States, Federal Reserve, Jun. 7, 2007.

2. Kiernan Davies, "Stocks and Profits," ABN AMRO report, Jul. 7, 2004.

3. Michael Santoli, "Rich America, Poor America," *Barron's*, Jan. 1, 2007.

4. David C. Johnson, "Income Gap Is Widening, Data Shows," *New York Times*, Mar. 29, 2007.

5. A recent presentation of this view was made by Barron's Economics Editor Gene Epstein in "The Great American Savings Myth," *Barron's*, May 28, 2007.

6. Johathan Stempel, "NASD Warns As Margin Debt Soars," Apr. 10, 2007, http://www.reuters.com.

7. Dan Ackman, "Retirement Doomsday," *Forbes*, Apr. 5, 2007.

8. David Malpass, "Running on Empty?" *Wall Street Journal*, March 29, 2005.

9. Michael Mandel, "Our Hidden Savings," *BusinessWeek*, Jan. 17, 2005.

10. Benjamin Friedman, *Day of Reckoning: The Consequences of American Economic Policy Under Reagan and After* (New York: Random House, 1988). Samuelson's comment is from the book's flap.

11. Alison Vershin, "Mortgages Push Late Loans to 17-Year High, FDIC Says," *Bloomberg*, Aug. 22, 2007.

12. Bill Gross, "Back to the Garden," www.pimco.com, July 2004.

13. Jonathan Clements, "Credit Problems: What to Do When You've Been Too Good," *Wall Street Journal*, Jan. 1, 2007.

14. April 2007 Senior Loan Officer Opinion Survey, Federal Reserve.

15. Mark Pittman, "Subprime Bondholders May Lose $75 Billion in U.S. Housing Slump," *Bloomberg*, Apr. 23, 2007.

16. Christine Haughney, "Troubles Hit Real Estate At High End." the *New York Times*, Mar. 10, 2007.

17. Robin Sidel and David Reilly, "No Worries: Banks Keeping Less Money in Reserve," *Wall Street Journal*, Feb. 27, 2007.

18. Examples include Andy Xie, "It's the Deficit, Stupid," Morgan Stanley, Aug. 31, 2006; Chris Giles, "BIS Warns Increasing Levels of Debt Are Creating Conditions for Financial Crises," *Financial Times*, June 28, 2005; Dan Roberts, "Warren Buffett Warns on U.S. Trade Deficit," *Financial Times,* Mar. 7, 2005; Paul Volker, "An Economy on Thin Ice," *The Washington Post*, Apr. 10, 2005.

19. Stephen Roach, "The Long Road," Morgan Stanley Report, May 14, 2004.

20. Stephen Roach, "In Search of Big Spenders," *Newsweek*, Sept. 11, 2006.

Chapter 3: Why the World Continues Lending (Most of Its Savings) to Us

1. In its periodical reports, the Bureau of Economic Analysis reports that our net international investment position stands near 2.5 trillion dollars compared with less than a trillion ten years ago.

2. Paul Volker, "An Economy on Thin Ice," *The Washington Post*, Apr. 10, 2005.

3. Paul Blustein, *And the Money Kept Rolling In (and Out): Wall Street, the IMF, and the Bankrupting of Argentina* (New York: Perseus Books, 2005), xx.

4. Robert Rubin, *In An Uncertain World* (New York: Random House, 2003), 30. Perhaps there is no clearer evidence that the United States remains the effective lender of last resort above organizations like the IMF and World Bank than the 1995 Mexico bailout package. At that time, the IMF lacked the tens of trillions in liquidity needed to reassure financial markets that the Mexican peso would be defended, and ultimately the White House had to provide the bulk of what ultimately was a massive $40 billion package. Clinton's decision to move ahead with the bailout plan, which was also supported by then Texas Governor George W. Bush, was very unpopular in Congress and among the public. But the move was a great success, as a complete disaster was averted, the Mexican economy recovered fairly rapidly, and all loans were ultimately paid off ahead of schedule.

5. Conrad Black, *Franklin Delano Roosevelt: Champion of Freedom* (New York: Perseus Books, 2003), 292.

6. Elliot Rosen, *Roosevelt, The Great Depression, and the Economics of Recovery* (Charlottesville, Va.: University of Virginia Press, 2005), 60.

7. Rosen, *Roosevelt,* 46; Robert Solomon, *The International Monetary System, 1945–1981* (New York: Harper & Row, 1982), 19; Barry Eichengreen, *Globalizing Capital: A History of the International Monetary System* (Princeton: Princeton University Press, 1996), 114.

8. William Silber, *When Washington Shut Down Wall Street: The Great Financial Crisis of 1914 and the Origins of America's Monetary Supremacy* (Princeton, NJ: Princeton Univ. Press, 2007), 90.

9. Solomon, *The International Monetary System,* 12.

10. Barry Eichengreen, *Golden Fetters: The Gold Standard and the Great Depression, 1919–1939* (New York: Oxford University Press, 1995), 395.

11. Solomon, *The International Monetary System,* 31.

12. Eichengreen, *Golden Fetters,* 395.

13. Solomon, *The International Monetary System*, 72.

14. Eichengreen, *Globalizing Capital*, 141.

15. William Greider, *Secrets of the Temple: How the Federal Reserve Runs the Country* (New York: Simon & Schuster, 1987), 344.

16. Greider, *Secrets of the Temple*, 187.

17. Robert Solomon, *Money on the Move: The Revolution in Finance Since 1980* (Princeton: Princeton University Press: 1999), 22.

18. Akio Mikuni and Taggart Murphy, *Japan's Policy Trap: Dollars, Deflation, and the Crisis of Japanese Finance* (Washington: Brookings Institution Press, 2002), xii.

19. Richard Duncan, "How Japan Financed Global Reflation," *FinanceAsia*, Feb. 2005.

Chapter 4: Relying on Foreigners: Our Economic Future May Be Out of Our Hands

1. Robert Solomon, *The International Monetary System, 1945–1981* (New York: Harper & Row, 1982), 31.

2. Debt growth is taken from the Flow of Funds Accounts of the United States, Federal Reserve, Jun. 7, 2007; GDP is provided by the Bureau of Economic Analysis.

3. U.S. international reserve levels are reported weekly by the U.S. Treasury.

4. Speech by Malcolm Knight, General Director at the Swiss National Bank/ Institute of International Economics Conference, Zurich, The Bank of International Settlements. Sept. 8, 2006, http://www.bis.org/speeches/sp060908.htm.

5. Robert Solomon, *Money on the Move: The Revolution in Finance Since 1980* (Princeton: Princeton University Press, 1999), 28.

6. Quoted from first page of W.P. Hogan and I.F. Pearce, *The Incredible Eurodollar* (London: George Allen & Unwin, 1982).

7. Sandra Ward, "Stuck in the Mush," *Barron's*, Sept. 13, 2004.

8. Randall Forsyth, "Party Like It's 1929," *Barron's*, Apr. 2, 2007.

9. While China holds well over one trillion dollars in foreign reserves, the precise composition of its holdings are not disclosed. However, considering the country's need to preserve a regulated exchange rate (and hence a weak yuan), it is known that the bulk of reserves are still maintained in dollars.

Chapter 5: Real Estate, this Decade's Economic Driver, Could Drive Us into Recession

1. Fact mentioned by National Association of Realtors Senior Economist Lawrence Yun, interview by Brian Louis, "Foreclosures Spur Ohio-Led States to Rescue Homes from Default," *Bloomberg*, May 16, 2007.

2. David Leonard, "What Statistics on Home Sales Aren't Saying," *New York Times*, Dec. 6, 2006.

3. Eve Mitchell, "Short Sales Spike Among Homeowners Stuck Holding 'Easy-Money' Loans," *Inside Bay Area*, May 13, 2007.

4. David Rosenberg, "The Ten Major Macro Themes of the Past Week," Merrill Lynch report, Sept. 8, 2006.

5. Ieva Augstums, "Mortgage Crisis' New Victims: 40,000 Workers This Year," *Austin American-Statesman*, Aug. 23, 2007, http://www.statesman.com/ business/content/business/stories/other/08/23/0823mortjobs.html.

6. Kathleen Howley, "Housing Slump in U.S. May Lead to First Drop Since Depression," *Bloomberg*, Sept. 17, 2006.

7. David Rosenberg, "Economic Commentary: Is This a Stable Backdrop?" Merrill Lynch Report, July 18, 2005.

8. Justin Lahart, "Why Investors Still Get Caught in the Subprime Trap," the *Wall Street Journal*, Feb. 22, 2007.

9. Kathleen Howley, "Housing 'Hangover' Kills Jobs as Spending Wanes; More Cuts Loom," *Bloomberg*, Feb. 21, 2007.

10. Michael Linderberger, "GM's Lutz Says Mortgage 'Meltdown' Hits Auto Sales," *Reuters*, Apr. 23, 2007, http://www.reuters.com.

11. Sandra Jones, "Spring Brings Record Fall," *Chicago Tribune*, May 10, 2007.

12. Source: U.S. Census Bureau.

13. W. Van Harlow, "The Equity You Live In: The Home as a Retirement Savings and Income Option," Fidelity Research Institute Report, Feb. 2007.

14. Chris Isadore, "Record Home Price Slump," Feb. 15, 2007, http://www.cnnmoney.com and Nancy Trejos, "Existing-Home Sales Fell Steeply," *The Washington Post*, Apr. 25, 2007.

15. "Housing Slump in U.S. May Lead to First Drop Since Depression," *Bloomberg*, Sept. 17, 2006.

16. Andy Laperriere, "Mortgage Meltdown," the *Wall Street Journal*, Mar. 21, 2007.

17. $718 billion was extracted from homes in 2005 alone. See Alan Greenspan and James Kennedy, FEDS working paper 2005–41 "Estimates of Home Mortgage Originations, Repayments, and Debt on One-to-Four Family Residences," Federal Reserve.

18. Bob Ivry, "Home Prices Fall in Rich New York Suburbs Once Immune to Slump," *Bloomberg*, May 8, 2007.

Chapter 6: The Negative Amortization Mortgage Loan Is Born

1. Dayana Yochim, "Need a Loan? No Problem," The Motley Fool Credit Center, May 2004, http://www.fool.com.

2. "Credit Card Mailings Take Usual First-Quarter Dip," *Direct Newsline*, May 25, 2004, http://enews.primediabusiness.com.

3. Mark Pittman, "Subprime Bondholders May Lose $75 Billion in U.S. Housing Slump," *Bloomberg,* Apr. 23, 2007.

4. Ibid.

5. Ruth Simon, James Hagerty, and James Areddy, "Housing-Bubble Talk Doesn't Scare Off Foreigners," the *Wall Street Journal*, Aug. 24, 2005.

6. Lynnley Browning, "The Subprime Loan Machine," the *New York Times*, Mar. 23, 2007.

7. Ibid.

8. Pittman, "Subprime Bondholders May Lose $75 Billion."

9. Ruth Simon, "Concerns Mount About Mortgage Risks," the *New York Times*, May 17, 2005.

10. Eve Mitchell, "Short Sales Spike Among Homeowners Stuck Holding 'Easy-Money' Loans," *Inside Bay Area*, May 13, 2007.

Chapter 7: Tighter Lending Standards and the Fed Can't Help

1. Remarks by John C. Dugan, Comptroller of the Currency, before an OCC Credit Risk Conference, Atlanta, Georgia, Oct. 27, 2005.

2. Allen Fishbein and Patrick Woodall, "Exotic or Toxic? An Examination of the Non-Traditional Mortgage Market for Consumers and Lenders," *Consumer Federation of America*, May 2006.

3. Kirstin Downey, "Regulators to Issue Mortgage Warning," *Washington Post*, Apr. 7, 2006.

4. Ruth Simon, "Mortgage Lenders Loosen Standards," *Wall Street Journal*, Jul. 26, 2005.

5. Downey, "Regulators to Issue Mortgage Warning."

6. Jody Shenn, "Subprime Meltdown Engulfs Even Borrowers with Good Credit," *Bloomberg*, Mar. 21, 2007.

7. Downey, "Regulators to Issue Mortgage Warning."

8. Bob Ivry, "Home Prices Fall in Rich New York Suburbs Once Immune to Slump," *Bloomberg*, May 8, 2007.

9. Joe Estrella, "Number of Listings in the Valley Hits a Record High," May 12, 2007, http://idahostatesman.com; David Fisher, "Filling in the Old Mill District," May 12, 2007, http://bendbulletin.com.

10. James Hagerty, "Mortgage Woes Force Banks To Take Hits to Sell Homes," *Wall Street Journal*, May 14, 2007.

11. Bill Gross, "Grim Reality," Pimco report, Apr. 2007, www.pimco.com.

12. Ibid.

Chapter 8: The Great American Equity Cash-Out Is Coming to an End

1. Alan Greenspan and James Kennedy, "Estimates of Home Mortgage Originations, Repayments, and Debt on One-to-Four Family Residences," FEDS working paper 2005–41.

2. Kenneth Harney, "Refinancing to Get Cash, Not Save It," *Washington Post*, Aug. 12, 2006.

3. Gene Sperling, "Housing Bust Meets the Equity-Withdrawal Blues," *Bloomberg*, Apr. 18, 2007.

4. Sperling, "Housing Bust Meets the Equity-Withdrawal Blues."

5. This was the level at the end of the first quarter of 2007. Source: Federal Reserve.

6. Robert Shiller and Karl Case, "Is There a Bubble in the Housing Market?" Brookings Paper (2003:2).

7. National Association of Realtors, as cited by David Rosenberg, "The 10 Major Macro Themes of the Past Week," Merrill Lynch report, May 11, 2007.

Chapter 9: Financial Culture Shock: Real Estate Can Have a Negative Return

1. Daniela Deane, "Middle Class Drives Soaring Purchases of Second Homes," *Washington Post*, Mar. 2, 2005.

2. Kemba Dunham, "Hot Condos, for Just a Letter," *Wall Street Journal*, May 19, 2005.

3. Robert Shiller and Karl Case, "Is There a Bubble in the Housing Market?" Brookings Paper (2003:2).

4. Sarah Max, "Don't Blow Your Home Equity," Apr. 22, 2004, http://cnnmoney.com.

5. Ibid.

6. Jonathan Clements, "Taking a Closer Look at Your Home's Return," *Wall Street Journal*, April 16, 2003.

7. Quoted in Jonathan Clements, "How to Stop Relatives From Bragging About Their Big Profits in Real Estate," *Wall Street Journal*, August 23, 2004.

8. W. Van Harlow, "The Equity You Live In: The Home as a Retirement Savings and Income Option," Fidelity Research Institute Report, Feb. 2007.

Chapter 10: Balance Sheet Recession: We Could Be Heading in a Japanese Direction

1. W.P. Hogan, and I.F. Pearce, *The Incredible Eurodollar* (London: George Allen & Unwin, 1982), 6.

2. Matthew Benjamin, "Most Americans Fear Recession in the Next 12 Months, Poll Finds," *Bloomberg*, Apr. 10, 2007; John Harwood, "NBC/WSJ Poll: Most Americans Are Worried about a Recession," Aug. 2, 2007, http://www.cnbc.com.

3. James Covert, "Retail-Sales Slide Fuels Concern," *Wall Street Journal*, May 11, 2007.

4. Damian Paletta and James Hagerty, "Foreclosure Level Reaches Record," *Wall Street Journal*, June 15, 2007.

5. Flow of Funds Accounts of the United States, Federal Reserve, June 7, 2007.

6. Henny Sender and Serena Ng, "Market Turmoil Tests Resistance of Buyout Boom," *Wall Street Journal*, June 8, 2007; Bernard Wysocki, "For Troubled Firms, A Flood of Big Loans," the *Wall Street Journal*, June 12, 2007.

7. Mark Whitehouse, "U.S. Consumers Cut Back on Borrowing," *Wall Street Journal*, June 8, 2007.

8. Lori Montgomery, "Stumping for Attention to Deficit Disorder," *Washington Post*, June 21, 2007.

9. Lawrence Meyer, *A Term at the Fed: The People and Policies of the World's Most Powerful Institution* (New York: Harper-Collins, 2004), 190.

10. John Kenneth Galbraith, *The Great Crash, 1929* (Cambridge, Mass: The Riverside Press, 1954), 75; Irving Fischer, "The Debt-Deflation Theory of Great Depressions," *Econometrica*, 1933.

11. Sandra Ward, "Downshifting Into Neutral on Stocks," *Barron's*, June 4, 2007.

12. Meyer, *A Term at the Fed*, xvi.

13. Meyer, *A Term at the Fed,* 189.

14. Christopher Wood, *The Bubble Economy: Japan's Extraordinary Speculative Boom of the 80's and the Dramatic Bust of the 90's* (New York: The Atlantic Monthly Press, 1992), 8.

15. Ibid.

16. Wood, *The Bubble Economy,* 4.

17. Meyer, *A Term at the Fed,* 187.

18. Milton Friedman and Anna Jacobson Schwartz, *A Monetary History of the United States, 1867–1960* (Princeton: Princeton University Press, 1963).

19. This is according to Peter Temin in *Did Monetary Forces Cause the Great Depression?* (Toronto: W.W. Norton & Co., 1976).

20. This is actually quoted from Milton Friedman and Anna Jacobson Schwartz, "Money and Business Cycles" in *Review of Economics and Statistics,* Feb. 1963, 45, which repeats their larger book's conclusion. Bank closures data is from Helen Burns, *The American Banking Community and New Deal Banking Reforms, 1933–1935* (London: Greenwood Press, 1974), 6.

21. Charles Kindleberger, *Manias, Panics and Crashes: A History of Financial Crises* (Hoboken, NJ: John Wiley & Sons, 2003), 112.

22. Galbraith, *The Great Crash,* 32.

23. Temin, *Did Monetary Forces Cause the Great Depression?*, 16.

24. Franklin D Roosevelt, *On Our Way* (New York: The John Day Co., 1934), 60.

25. Ben Bernanke, "Nonmonetary Effects of the Financial Crisis in the Propagation of the Great Depression," in *Essays on the Great Depression* (Princeton: Princeton University Press, 2000), 47; Robert McElvaine, *The Great Depression* (New York: Times Books, 1984), 41.

26. Melchior Palyi, *The Twilight of Gold 1914–1936: Myths and Realities* (Chicago: Henry Regnery, 1972), 208.

27. Richard Koo, *Balance Sheet Recession: Japan's Struggle with Unchartered Economics and its Global Implications* (Hoboken, NJ: John Wiley & Sons, 2003), 42 and 47.

28. Koo, *Balance Sheet Recession,* 40.

Chapter 11: Smiling on the Lawnmower: Affluent Poverty

1. Gene Epstein, "The Great American Savings Myth," *Barron's,* May 28, 2007.

2. As of the June 2007, the Mortgage Bankers Association was expecting foreclosures to continue rising into 2008. See Damian Paletta and James Hagerty, "Foreclosure Level Reaches Record," the *Wall Street Journal,* June 15, 2007.

3. Matthew Benjamin and Aliza Marcus, "Americans without Health Benefits Rose to 47 Million," *Bloomberg,* Aug. 28, 2007.

4. Jonathan Clements, "When Retirement Experts Talk, Why Doesn't Anybody Listen?" *Wall Street Journal,* June 20, 2007.

5. Press release from Hewitt Associates, "Hewitt Study Shows Nearly Half of U.S. Workers Cash Out of 401(k) Plans When Leaving Jobs," July 25, 2005.

6. Jonathan Clements, "The Debt Bubble Threatens to Derail Many Baby Boomers' Retirement Plans," the *Wall Street Journal,* Mar. 8, 2006; Flow of Funds Accounts of the United States, Federal Reserve, June 7, 2007.

7. Flow of Funds Accounts of the United States, Federal Reserve.

8. David Cay Johnson, "Income Gap Is Widening, Data Shows," *New York Times,* Mar. 29, 2007.

9. Frank Levy and Peter Temin, "Inequality and Institutions in 20th Century America," Massachusetts Institute of Technology, Working Paper 07-17 (May 1, 2007).

10. Johnson, "Income Gap Is Widening."

11. Robert Frank, "Maybe the Rich Really Are Like Us—In Debt," *Wall Street Journal,* May 5, 2007.

12. David Leonhardt, "Can't Sell Your Home? Maybe It's Priced Too Low,"*New York Times*, Jul. 11, 2007; Vikas Bajaj; "Increasing Rate of Foreclosures Upsets Atlanta," *New York Times*, Jul. 9, 2007.

13. Sandra Ward, "The Big Hook" (interview with Lee Mikles and Mark Miller), *Barron's*, Sept. 5, 2005.

14. Data taken from Bill Gross, "Looking for Contagion in All the Wrong Places," Pimco Report, July, 2007, www.pimco.com.

Chapter 12: As the Fed Cuts Rates This Time, Could the Dollar Finally Collapse?

1. Raymond Moley, *After Seven Years* (New York: Harper & Brothers Publishers, 1939), 152.

2. Anthony Solomon, *The Dollar, Debt and the Trade Deficit* (New York: New York University Press, 1987), 42.

3. Ron Suskind, *The Price of Loyalty: George W. Bush, the White House, and the Education of Paul O'Neill* (New York: Simon & Schuster, 2004), 291.

4. William Greider, *Secrets of the Temple: How the Federal Reserve Runs the Country* (New York: Simon & Schuster, 1987), 593.

5. Ibid.

6. Barry Eichengreen, "Why the Dollar's Fall Is Not to Be Welcomed," *Financial Times*, Dec. 20, 2004.

7. Andrew Browne, "China's Next Export Could Be Inflation as Its Own Costs Rise," the *Wall Street Journal*, Nov. 8, 2004.

8. Robert Rubin, *In an Uncertain World* (New York: Random House, 2003), 183.

9. Quoted in William Pesek, "U.S. Rogue Nation Image Hurts Dollar in Asia," *Bloomberg*, Dec. 19, 2004.

10. Robert Solomon, *Money on the Move: The Revolution in Finance since 1980* (Princeton: Princeton University Press: 1999), 23.

Chapter 13: Why the Time Is Right for Gold to Skyrocket

1. These keen observations about gold's nature were originally made by Timothy Green in *The New World of Gold* (New York: Walker Publishing Company, 1981), xvi–xvii.

2. Milton Friedman, *Money Mischief: Episodes in Monetary History* (New York: Harcourt Brace Jovanovich, 1992), 193.

3. Peter Bernstein, *The Power of Gold: The History of an Obsession* (New York: John Wiley & Sons, 2000), 5.

4. By closing down the stock exchange, the Treasury secretary effectively prevented Europeans, who held substantial investments in American equities, from selling their stock and converting received dollars into gold to be shipped home. See William Silber, *When Washington Shut Down Wall Street: The Great Financial Crisis of 1914 and the Origins of America's Monetary Supremacy* (Princeton, NJ: Princeton University Press, 2007), 90.

5. This statistic on the amount of U.S. currency circulating outside the United States is from "The Use and Counterfeiting of United States Currency Abroad," Department of the U.S. Treasury, Sept. 2006.

6. Sam Nagarajan, "India RBI to Cap Rupee Gains, Essar's Paramsivam Says," *Bloomberg*, Aug. 8, 2007.

7. Jonathan Stempel, "NASD Warns As Margin Debt Soars," Apr. 10, 2007, http://www.reuters.com.

8. Gerard Minack, "Party Like it's 1999," *Morgan Stanley report*, Nov. 24, 2006.

9. Source: Bank of International Settlements.

10. Roger Lowenstein, *When Genius Failed: The Rise and Fall of Long-Term Capital Management* (New York: Random House, 2000), 104 and 191.

11. Towards Greater Financial Stability: A Private Sector Perspective, The Report of the Counterparty Risk Management Group II, July 27, 2005, http://www.crmpolicygroup.org, 121–2.

12. Ibid, 124.

13. Ibid, b-3 and passim.

14. Gillian Tett, "Derivatives Boom Has Created Instability, says ECB President," *Financial Times*, Jan. 29, 2007.

15. Carrick Mollenkamp, "Credit Derivatives May Pose Risk For Investors, IMF Report Says," *Wall Street Journal*, Apr. 6, 2005.

16. Justin Lahart and Aaron Lucchetti, "Wall Street Fears Bear Stearns Is Tip Of An Iceberg," *Wall Street Journal*, June 25, 2007; Financial Stability Report, Bank of England, April 2007.

17. Lahart and Luchett, "Wall Street Fears Bear Stearns Is Tip of an Iceberg."

18. Bill Gross, "Looking for Contagion in all the Wrong Places," Jul. 2007, www.pimco.com

19. Kelly, Kate and Serena Ng, "Bear Stearns Bails Out Fund with Big Loan," *Wall Street Journal*, Jun. 26–27, 2007.

20. Bob Woodward, *Maestro: Greenspan's Fed and the American Boom* (New York: Simon & Schuster, 2000), 37. Woodward points out that under a loosely-worded provision in Section 13 of the Federal Reserve Act, the Fed, with the agreement of five out of seven Board members, can lend to institutions other than banks. It is not clear if the Fed has actually ever done this.

21. Mark Bruno, "Institutions Continue To Drop U.S. Equities," *Pensions & Investments*, Jul. 9, 2007.

22. Lukanyo Mnyanda, "Dollar is 'Vulnerable' to Drop in Investment Inflows, BIS Says," *Bloomberg*, Jun. 24, 2007.

23. Richard Bookstaber, *A Demon of Our Own Design: Markets, Hedge Funds, and the Perils of Financial Innovation* (Hoboken, NJ: John Wiley & Sons, 2007), 145.

24. Ibid.

25. Sharmila Whelan, "China Monetary—Out of Control?" CLSA report, Jul. 13, 2007.

26. Paul McCulley, "What Can Go Wrong: China," June 2007, www.pimco.com.

27. Andy Xie, "Disaster in the Air?" *South China Morning Post*, May 11, 2007.

28. Dong Tao, "China Economics: What If Inflation Hits 8%?" Credit Suisse report, Jul. 31, 2007.

29. Jane Spencer, "China Pays Steep Price as Textile Exports Boom," *Wall Street Journal*, Aug. 22, 2007.

30. Ibid.

31. Joanna Slater, "World's Assets Hit Record Value of $140 Trillion," *Wall Street Journal*, Jan. 1, 2007.

32. Bookstaber, *A Demon of Our Own Design*, 170.

33. Barton Biggs, *Hedge Hogging* (Hoboken, NJ: John Wiley & Sons, 2006), 264.

Chapter 14: Stocks and Bonds Offer Little Compensation for Risk Today

1. William Greider, *Secrets of the Temple: How the Federal Reserve Runs the Country* (New York: Simon & Schuster, 1987), 460.

2. Steven Rattner, "The Coming Credit Meltdown," *Wall Street Journal*, Jun. 18, 2007.

3. Robert Rodriguez, speech before the CFA Society of Chicago, Jun. 28, 2007, http://www.fpafunds.com/news_070703_absense_of_fear.htm.

4. Though well known, these points were made by David Leonhardt in "Some Rain on the Parade on Wall St.," *New York Times*, Jul, 11, 2007.

5. Gerard Minack, "The Offshore Get-Out," Morgan Stanley report, Jan. 15, 2007.

6. David Leonhardt, "A Classic Investing Theory," *New York Times*, Aug. 15, 2007.

7. Nick Baker and Daniel Hauck, "Wall Street Analysts More Bearish Than Ever; More Accurate, Too," *Bloomberg*, Jun. 17, 2007.

8. Spencer Jakab, "Boomer Effect: Gloomy Forecasts," *Wall Street Journal*, Mar. 28, 2007.

9. Ibid.

10. William Bulkeley, "IBM To Add Some Debt To Boost Stock Buybacks," *Wall Street Journal,* Apr. 25, 2007; Lisa Rapaport, "Johnson & Johnson to Start $10 Billion Share Buyback," *Bloomberg,* Jul. 9, 2007.

11. Justin Lahart, "Shares Head To The Sidelines: At What Cost?" *The Wall Street Journal,* Apr. 9, 2007.

12. Interview on CNBC cable television, Aug. 15, 2007.

13. Lina Saigol and James Politi, "M&A Volume Tops $1,000Bn," *Financial Times,* Mar. 3, 2007.

14. Dennis Berman, Servena Ng and Gina Chon, "Banks Delay Sale of Chrysler Debt as Market Stalls," *The Wall Street Journal,* Jul. 26, 2007.

15. Paul Davies and Saskia Scholtes, "Chrysler In Trouble Over Debt Take-Up," *Financial Times,* Jul. 26, 2007.

16. Ibid.

17. Lacy Hunt, "Quarterly Review and Outlook," Hoisington Investment Management Report, Second Quarter 2007.

18. George Wehrfritz and Jonathan Adams, "Higher and Mightier," *Newsweek,* Jul. 16, 2007; Song Jung-a, "South Korea's State Pension Fund Dips Toe in World of Risk," *Financial Times,* Jul. 13, 2007; Jason Singer et al, "Governments Get Bolder in Buying Equity Stakes," *Wall Street Journal,* Jul. 24, 2007.

19. Barton Biggs, "The Spooky Echoes of '87," *Newsweek,* Jul. 16, 2007.

20. Roger Lowenstein, *Buffett: The Making of an American Capitalist* (New York: Random House, 1995), 94, 114.

21. Ibid, 118.

Chapter 15: Gold's Scarcity: New Sources of Demand and Falling Supply

1. Though a simple calculation, this precise point illustrating the small size of the gold market in relation with financial markets came from Paul Mylchreest, when he was still an analyst at Cheuvreux in London, in a brilliant report entitled, "Remonetization of Gold: Start Hoarding", Cheuvreux report, Jan. 2006, 9. The figure on gold in existence came from GFMS, which provided much of the data from this chapter. The calculations are based on gold at $665 an ounce and annual gold mining supply of roughly 2,500 tons.

2. Holly Watt and Robert Winnett, "Goldfinger Brown's £2 Billion Blunder in the Bullion Market," *Sunday Times,* Apr. 15, 2007.

3. Barry Eichengreen, *Golden Fetters: The Gold Standard and the Great Depression, 1919–1939* (New York: Oxford University Press, 1995), 116.

4. The $10 trillion figure is based on the Fed's last report of M3, the broadest monetary measure, which was discontinued in 2006 for reasons that are not completely

clear. Although the latest figure is not available, it is evidently larger than the 2006 amount reported. M2, which is still reported and is a narrower measure of our money stock, is worth over $7 trillion.

5. Greenspan's quotation is from Holly Watt and Robert Winnett, "Goldfinger Brown's £2 Billion Blunder in the Bullion Market," *Sunday Times*, Apr. 15, 2007.

6. Source: International Monetary Fund.

7. Pham-Duy Nguyen and Claudia Carpenter, "Gold Rises After European Central Bank Caps Sales," *Bloomberg*, Jun. 1, 2007.

8. Neal Ryan, "Central Banks Are Becoming Gold Buyers, Blanchard & Co. Says," Feb. 7, 2007, www.gata.org.

9. Danielle Rossingh, "Russia's Central Bank May Double Gold, Official Says," *Bloomberg*, Nov. 15, 2005.

10. Ambrose Evans-Pritchard, "Fears Over Treasury Losing Control of Gold Left in Its Vaults," Apr. 17, 2007, www.telegraph.co.uk.

11. Jon Bergtheil et al, "Global Mining Strategy," J.P. Morgan report, Feb. 7, 2007.

12. Andrea Cheung et al, *Gold Book*, BMO Capital Markets Research, Feb. 2007; Bergtheil et al., "Global Markets Strategy."

13. Source: World Gold Council.

14. Source: GFMS.

15. Natalie Dempster, "The Role of Gold in India," World Gold Council Report, Sept. 2006.

16. Ibid.

17. Lu Hui, "Exchange Starts Gold Trading Via Local Banks," Jun. 26, 2007, www.chinaview.cn.

18. Source: exchangetradedgold.com.

19. Ibid.

Chapter 16: When You Simply Want Financial Insurance

1. The number of collectors was taken from David Bowers, *The Expert's Guide to Collecting & Investing in Rare Coins* (Atlanta, GA: Whitman Publishing, 2005), 26. He points out that *A Guide Book of United States Coins* is among the ten best-selling nonfiction titles of all time.

2. "1920-S $10 Realizes $1,725,000 At Auction," pcgs.com, Apr. 6, 2007.

Chapter 17: Mining Stocks, ETFs, and GoldMoney

1. Michael Jalonen, "Gold & Precious Metals Weekly," Merrill Lynch report, Jun. 25, 2007.

2. Scott Patterson, "Finally, Miners May Join the Gold Rush," *Wall Street Journal*, May 10, 2007.

3. This quotation was found by Douglas Goold and Andrew Willis as shown in *The Bre-X Scandal* (Toronto: McClelland & Stewart Inc., 1997), 263.

4. These details on the Bre-X story are from Douglas Goold and Andrew Willis' brilliant book, *The Bre-X Scandal* (Toronto: McClelland & Stewart Inc., 1997).

5. Craig Karmin, "Would You Like to Pay by Check, Cash—Or Gold?" *Wall Street Journal*, Oct. 8–9, 2005.

Chapter 18: Rare Coins: A Bet on the Highest Possible Gains in Gold

1. Quoted from Alison Frankel, *Double Eagle: The Epic Story of the World's Most Valuable Coin* (New York: W.W. Norton & Company, 2006), 46.

2. Alan Greenspan, "Gold and Economic Freedom" in Ayn Rand, *Capitalism: The Unknown Ideal* (Chicago: Signet, 1962), 107.

3. Frankel, *Double Eagle*, 48.

4. David Bowers, *The Expert's Guide to Collecting & Investing in Rare Coins* (Atlanta, GA: Whitman Publishing, 2005), 8–9.

5. Robert Motherwell, "A $20 Gold Coin—For $1.9 Million," *Wall Street Journal*, Feb. 24, 2006.

6. Scott Travers, *Rare Coin Investment Strategy* (New York: Simon & Schuster, 1986), 6.

7. A great book in which to see images of the 1933 Double Eagle as well as other spectacular American rare coins is Jeff Garrett and Ron Guth's *100 Greatest U.S. Coins* (Atlanta, GA: Whitman Publishing, 2nd ed. 2005).

8. Coin dealers are not required to report their activity to the U.S. government, making a solid estimate of the coin market's size impossible. David Bowers, one of the authorities on the gold market, speculates (which is all one can do) that as much as $500 million could trade annually in the American coin market, but he included bullion coins in this figure, which dominate sales. Bowers, *The Expert's Guide*, 30.

9. Ibid, 484.

Chapter 19: Why Silver Might Rise More Than Gold

1. Stephen Fay, *Beyond Greed: How the Two Richest Families in the World, the Hunts of Texas and the House of Saud, Tried to Corner the Silver Market* (New York: Viking Press, 1982).

2. Source: The Silver Institute.

3. David Morgan, *Get The Skinny on Silver Investing* (Garden City, NY: Morgan James Publishing, 2006), 20. You can find out more about investing in silver at his website, Silver-Investor.com; Milton Friedman, "FDR, Silver and China" in *Money Mischief: Episodes in Monetary History* (New York: Harcourt Brace Jovanovich, 1992), 157.

4. Source: The Silver Institute.

5. Morgan, *Get The Skinny*, 21.

6. Ibid, 18.

Conclusion: Don't Be A Gold Bug: Sell When It Is Time To Sell

1. John Kenneth Galbraith, *The Affluent Society* (Cambridge, Mass: The Riverside Press, 1958).

2. Ibid, 8.

3. Richard McGregor, "Beijing Freezes State-Controlled Prices As Inflation Fuels Discord," *Financial Times*, Sept. 20, 2007.

4. Steven Weisman, "Paulson Warns Against Legislation on China," *New York Times*, Sept. 11, 2007.

5. Martin Wolf, "America Is Now on the Comfortable Path to Ruin," *Financial Times*, Aug. 17, 2004.

6. Kathleen Howley, "Realtors Cut Forecast, Say Slump Will Extend to 2008," *Bloomberg*, Sept. 11, 2007.

Index

A

Adjustable rate mortgages, 53–56, 58, 92
Affluent poverty, 87–93, 104
AltA mortgages, 49
American Buffalo coins, 149, 150, 153, 156
American Eagle coins, 149, 155
American Liberty coins, 155
AngloGold, 160
Argentina, 25, 114
Atlanta, GA, 91
Australia:
    gold coins of, 153–154
    gold mining in, 143
    sovereign funds and, 134
Austria, 153
Automated underwriting, 55
Automobile industry, benefits and, 82
Automobile sales, equity withdrawal and, 47–48

B

Baby boomers, stock portfolio liquidation and,
    132, 195
Balance sheet recession:
    Japan and, 81–85
    U.S. and, 75–81, 85–86, 104
Balance Sheet Recession (Koo), 84

Bank of America, 92
Bank of England, 138–139, 143
Bank of France, 139
Bank of International Settlements, 194
Bank of Japan, 31, 33, 83, 84
Barclays, 134
Barnes, Martin, 38
Barrick Gold Corporation, 160
Barron's, 92
Bear Stearns Companies Inc., 119
Bernanke, Ben:
    China and, 39
    entitlements and, 12, 13, 14
    on Great Depression, 84
    inflation and, 85, 192, 196
Bernstein, Peter, 112
Bid-ask spread, of rare coins, 175
Biggs, Barton, 125, 134
BMO Financial Group, 143
Bonds:
    compared to store of gold, 137–138
    securitized mortgages and, 54–55, 76
    U.S. Treasury, 26, 60, 128–129
    valuation and current risk, 117
    weak U.S. dollar and, 123
Bookstaber, Richard, 121, 123
Boots, 133

Bowers, David, 170, 176
Brazil:
    economy of, 133
    exchange rate and, 40
    international reserves of, 194
Bre-X, 160–161
Bretton Woods Agreement, 28–30
Bretton Woods II, 38, 87, 194
BRIC countries, 133
Brown, Gordon, 140
Buffett, Warren:
    silver and, 188
    stocks in 1969 and, 7, 135
Bullion, buying gold as, 149–158
Bundesbank, 30
Burns, Arthur, 30
Bush administration, 98–99, 101
Business Week, 110
Buy backs, of stock, 131–132

C

Canada:
    economy of, 133
    exchange rate and, 28
    gold coins of, 149
Cash flow deficit, of U.S. households, 79–80
Cash-out proceeds, *see* Equity extraction
Central Bank Gold Agreements, 141
Central banks, *see also* Federal Reserve Board;
        specific countries
    gold supply and, 138–143
    mortgage securitization and, 55
    U.S. currency versus gold and, 4–6
    U.S. dollar and, 113–116, 194–195
Cerberus Capital Management, 133
Certification, of coins, 155, 177, 179
Challenger, Gray & Christmas Inc., 47
Cheney, Richard, 99
China:
    consumption as percent of economy, 21
    demand for gold in, 144–145
    global economy and, 133, 134
    gold coins of, 153
    gold reserves and, 6, 142
    inflation and, 101
    international reserves of, 36–37, 87–88
    silver and, 189
    U.S. dollar and, 102–103, 121–123, 193–194
Chrysler, 133
Coins, gold, 149–151, 166–167. *See also* Rare coins

buying on Internet, 153–158
    as percentage of portfolio, 151–153
Commodity futures, gold purchases and, 166
Common date coins, 167, 171–175
Confiscatable gold, 169–170
Connally, John, 30
Consumer spending, equity withdrawal and,
        46–47, 63–66
Corporate debt, 77
Corporate profits:
    current, 130–131
    from financial activities, 19
Corrigan, Gerald, 118
Counterparty risk, 110, 112
Countrywide Financial Corp., 4, 47
Credit Suisse, 122
Cruise, Christopher, 59
Current account deficit:
    balance sheet recession and, 77–78
    Gold Standard, monetary policy and growth
        of, 23–33
    international reserves and, 35–42

D

Daimler Chrysler, 133
de Gaulle, Charles, 2
Dealers, in gold, 176, 180
    finding and working with, 157–158
Debt, *see* Household debt; Mortgage debt;
        U.S. national debt
"Debt-Deflation Theory of the Great
        Depression" (Fisher), 79
Deflation:
    Federal Reserve's concern about, 95–96, 196
    in Japan, 81–85
    possible in U.S., 85–86, 96
Deliveries, of gold, 156
Demon of Our Own Design, A (Bookstaber), 121
Depression, possibility of, 195
Derivatives, potential market failure and gold
        rally, 117–121
Devaluation, effect of possible U.S. dollar,
        98–106, 192–197
Digital gold, 163–166
Dodd, David, 130–131
Double Eagle coins, 172, 174, 181
Dow Jones Industrial Average:
    gain in, from 1982–2007, 19, 128
    gold's performance versus, 110–112
    rare coins index versus, 170

Down payments, debt levels and, 53–54, 58
DRDGOLD, 164
Duckor, Dr. Steven, 155
Dugan, John, 57–58
Duncan, Richard, 33
DXY index, 97

E

Earnings per share, current corporate, 130–131
Ebay, 154
Economic growth:
  interest rates and dollar's value, 95–106
  possibility of U.S. recession and, 75–86
  in U.S. versus world, 97, 133
Economist, The, 98
Eichengreen, Barry, 100
England, central bank of, 138–139
Entitlement programs, federal deficit and,
  12–14, 195–196
Epstein, Gene, 89
Equity extraction:
  balance sheet recession and, 80
  for consumer spending, 46–47, 63–66
  for investments/second homes, 67–71
Essays on the Great Depression (Bernanke), 84
Euro, 196
Europe, see also specific countries
  consumption as percent of economy, 21
  exchange rate and, 40
Exchange rates, 28, 40, 196
Exchange-traded funds:
  gold and, 6, 145, 161–163, 166
  silver and, 190
Expert's Guide to Collecting & Investing in Rare
  Coins (Bowers), 176

F

Fannie Mae, 54
FastQual automated loan approvals, 55
Federal Reserve Board:
  Flow of Funds report, 90–91, 104
  gold reserves and, 140
  Great Depression and, 83–84
  illiquid markets and, 119–121
  interest rates and 9/11 attacks, 88
  interest rates and balance sheet recession,
    79–81
  interest rates and mortgages rates, 50, 54,
    59–60

interest rates and U.S. dollar, 192–195
Long Term Capital Management and,
  118, 120
Financial markets, size of U.S., 25–26
Financial Times, 98
Fisher, Irving, 79, 85
Foreclosures, 89, 92
Foreign central banks, see Central banks
Foreign currency reserves, 101, 113–116
Fort Knox, 137–138
France:
  central bank of, 139
  exchange rate and, 28
  gold holdings of, 142
  gold standard and, 29
Freddie Mac, 54
Friedman, Benjamin, 19
Friedman, Milton, 83, 110
Futures, gold purchases and, 166

G

Galbraith, John Kenneth, 191–192
Ganz, David, 170
GDP (gross domestic product), global
  debt and, 116
  U.S. and, 133–135
  world trade imbalances and, 95–106
GDP (gross domestic product), U.S.
  derivatives and, 117
  household debt and, 15–16, 21, 77
  housing-related activity and, 47
  national debt and, 2–5, 12, 24, 99–100, 105
Gemici, Alex, 58–59
General Motors, 47
Generation X, negative savings rate of, 132
Generic coins, 171–175
Germany:
  central bank of, 30
  gold and, 5, 142
GFMS Limited, 144
GLD (State Street Global Advisors), 161–162
Global economy, see GDP (gross domestic
  product), global
Global Financial Stability Report (IMF), 118
Global Insight, Inc., 144
Gold, in general:
  average cost of producing ounce of,
    143–144
  as historical measure of value, 1–2, 27–30,
    110–113, 197–198

Gold, in general (*continued*)
  performance versus Dow Jones Industrial
    Average, 110–112
  physical characteristics of, 109
  strength versus currency markets, 5–6
Gold Anti-Trust Action Committee
  (GATA), 143
Gold, catalysts for price rally of, 113–125
  China's economy and, 121–123
  derivatives and, 117–121
  lack of alternative investment and, 116–117
  paper currencies and, 113–116
Gold, supply of and demand for, 123–125,
  137–145
  central banks supply of, 138–143
  industry demand for, 138, 144
  investment demand for, 138, 144–145
  jewelry demand for, 138, 144
  mine production of, 138, 143–144
  recycled (scrap) supply of, 138–139
Gold Reserve Act of 1934, 170
Gold, ways to buy:
  coins, 149–151, 153–158, 166
  digital, 163–166
  exchange traded funds, 6, 145,
    161–163, 166
  on Internet, 153–158
  jewelry, 167
  mining stocks, 159–161, 166
  rare coins, 150, 167, 169–185
Goldgrams, 164
Goldman Sachs, 64
GoldMoney, 163–166
Grading of coins, 157, 171, 177–178
Graham, Benjamin, 130–131
Great Depression, The, 26, 85, 169, 192
  Bernanke on, 84
  Federal Reserve's role in, 83–84
Greece, 142
Greenspan, Alan:
  on gold market, 137
  hidden confiscation of wealth, 169
  mortgage equity withdrawal and, 64
  stock market and, 76
  tax cuts and, 88
  on value of gold, 140
Gross, Bill, 60, 119
Gross domestic product, *see* GDP (gross
  domestic product)
Grupo México, 124
Guandong Galanz Enterprise, 101

H

Haggling, price of gold purchase and,
  157–158
Hambro, Peter, 143
Health insurance, lack of, 89
Hedge funds, *see* Derivatives
Helvetia, 177
High-end rare coins, 180–181
High-Grade Credit Strategies Enhanced
  Leverage Fund, 119
High-Grade Structured Credit Strategies
  Fund, 119
High-yield bonds, 129
Hogan, W.P., 75
Home values:
  debt levels and affluent poverty, 87–93
  fall in, 195
  improvements and, 68–69
  U.S. economy and, 45–52
  wages and traditional rise in, 53–54
House of Saud, 188
Household debt, *see also* Mortgage debt
  versus assets, affluent poverty and, 87–93
  balance sheet recession and, 78
  rise of, 3, 5, 76
  slow income growth and low savings rates,
    15–21
Hunt family, 188
Hunt, Lacy, 133

I

Iacocca, Lee, 99
IAMGOLD, 164
IBM, 132
Income inequality, 16
Incredible Eurodollar, The (Hogan and
  Pearce), 75
India:
  demand for gold in, 6, 144
  economy of, 133
  exchange rate and, 40
  international reserves of, 115–116, 194
  rupee's value and, 115–116
  silver and, 189
Indian Head coins, 155, 171, 172, 173, 177
Industrial demand:
  for gold, 138, 144
  for silver, 189–190

Inflation:
  in China, U.S. dollar and, 121–123
  gold as protection against, 110
  gold prices and, 140
  interest rates and, 96–97, 128–129, 196
Interest rates:
  balance sheet recession and, 79–81
  dollar's international value and, 95–106
  Federal Reserve and, 50, 54, 59–60, 79–81,
    88, 192–195
  inflation and, 96–97, 128–129, 196
  Japanese deflation and, 83, 84
International Gold Bullion Exchange, 164
International Monetary Fund:
  Global Financial Stability Report, 118, 194
  gold holdings of, 142
International monetary system:
  reserves and, 35–42
  vendor financing system and, 4
  Wittenveen on, 38
Internet:
  advantages of using, 157
  buying gold on, 153–158
  rare coins and, 176, 183–185
Investment demand, for gold, 138, 144–145
Ireland, 88
iShares Silver Trust (SLV), 190
Italy, 142, 196

J

Japan:
  central bank of, 31, 33, 83, 84
  consumption as percent of economy, 21
  deflation in, 81–85, 116
  gold reserves and, 6, 142
  interest rates and, 105
  international reserves of, 32–33, 87–88, 194
  U.S. dollar and, 102–103
Japan's Policy Trap (Mikuni and Murphy), 32
Jewelry:
  demand for gold and, 138, 144
  as way to buy gold, 167
Jobs, see also Wages/salaries
  sluggish growth of, 19, 20–21, 76
  tied to real estate industry, 47
Johnson & Johnson, 132
Johnson, Lyndon B., 29
Joint Center for Housing Studies, at
    Harvard, 47
J.P. Morgan, 143

K

Kangaroo coins, 153
Kennedy, Jim, 64
Kindleberger, Charles, 51
Knight, Malcolm, 37
Koo, Richard, 84
Kotlikoff, Lawrence, 13
Kruggerands, 149, 153

L

LendingTree, 63–64
Leonhardt, David, 130
Leuthold, Steven, 79
Leveraged investment strategies, potential for
    gold rally and, 117–121
Liberty Head coins, 172, 173, 177
Long Term Capital Management (LTCM),
    117–118, 120
Low documentation loans, 50, 58

M

Mail, coin delivery and, 156
Malpass, David, 17
Manias, Panics, and Crashes (Kindleberger), 51
Maple Leaf coin, 149
Mayer, Chris, 68–69
McAdoo, William, 112
McCulley, Paul, 122
Mergers and acquisitions, share prices and, 131,
    132–133
Mexico:
  economic crisis in, 25, 114
  exchange rate and, 40
  global economy and, 133
Meyer, Lawrence, 81–82
Mikuni, Alio, 32
Milwaukee, WI, 68
Minack, Gerard, 64, 117
Mining:
  of gold, 138, 143–144
  of silver, 189
Mining stocks, 159–161, 166
Mints, coin issues of, 155, 178
Monetary History of the United States, 1876–1960,
    A (Friedman and Schwartz), 83
Morgan, David, 189
Morgan Silver Dollar, 172, 173, 177–179
Mortgage debt, see also Household debt
  compared to home values, 90

Mortgage debt, (*continued*)
  defaults and foreclosures on, 46
  increased with equity withdrawal, 63–71
  negative amortization and, 53–56
  securitization of, 54–55
  subprime, 4, 20, 49–59, 119
  tightened lending standards and, 57–59
Mortgage equity withdrawal (MEW):
  balance sheet recession and, 80
  for consumer spending, 46–47, 63–66
  for investments/second homes, 67–71
Murphy, Taggart, 32

N

National Association of Realtors, 49
Negative amortization, 53–56
New Century Financial, 55
New York, NY, 91
Newmont Mining Corporation, 160
Newsweek, 98
Niemira, Michael, 75–76
Nixon, Richard, 29–30, 110
Nugget coin, 154
Numismatic Guaranty Corporation (NGC),
  157, 178, 185

O

Office of the Comptroller of the
  Currency, 20
O'Neill, Paul, 99

P

Pakistan, 129
Panda coin, 153
Paradox of thrift, 19
Paulson, Henry, 193
Peace Silver Dollar, 172, 173
Pearce, I.F., 75
Philadelphia Gold & Silver Index
  (XAU), 159
Philarmonics coin, 153
Philippines, 142
Pick-a-payment mortgages, 53–56
Plaza Accord of 1985, 102
Plutonomy, 16
Portfolio, percentage of gold in, 151–153
Poverty, affluent, 87–93, 104
Professional Coin Grading Service (PCGS),
  157, 178, 185

Q

Quinlan, Joseph, 102

R

Rare coins, 150, 167, 169–185
  advantages of investing in, 181–185
  certification of, 155, 177, 179
  common or generic date, 167, 171–175
  confiscation risk and, 169–170
  grading system for, 157, 171
  list of exceptionally rare coins, 182
  patience and value of, 170–171, 175–176
  tips for investing in, 175–181
Rattner, Steven, 129
Reagan, Ronald, 31
Real estate:
  equity extraction for consumer spending,
    46–47, 63–66
  equity extraction for improvements/vacation
    homes, 67–71
  home values and U.S. economy, 45–52,
    87–93, 195
  savings and investments in, 18
Recession, *see also* Balance sheet recession
  expectations of, 75–81
  fall of currency values and, 113, 116
  of past, 127–128
  real estate and estimated probability of,
    45–52
Recycled (scrap) supply of gold, 138–139
Refinancing, 64. *See also* Mortgage equity
    withdrawal (MEW)
Reich, John, 58
Rental yields, 70–71
"Report of the Counterparty Risk Management
    Policy Group II," 118
Retirement savings, lack of, 89
Risk:
  bond yields and current, 128–129
  gold and, 110, 112, 151–153
  stock valuations and current, 130–135
Roach, Stephen, 21, 88
Rodriguez, Robert, 129, 134–135
Rooms-To-Go, 19
Roosevelt, Franklin D., 26, 83, 85, 169, 192
Rosenberg, David, 51
Ross, Wilbur, 132
Rubin, Robert, 101
Rupee, 115–116

Russia:
  economy of, 133
  foreign investment and, 25
  gold reserves and, 6, 142
  international reserves of, 36–37, 87–88, 194
  sovereign funds and, 134
  U.S. dollar and, 103

S

S&P 500 Index, 130
Safety deposit boxes, gold storage and, 152
Salaries, *see* Wages/salaries
Salomon, Anthony, 98
Samuelson, Paul, 19
San Francisco, CA, 45–46, 56, 68, 91
Sanluis, 124
Savings rates:
  domestic, 17–18, 20–21, 31, 195
  foreign, 24–25
Schwartz, Anna J., 83
Second homes, equity extraction and real estate
     values, 67–71
Securitization, of mortgage loans, 54–55
Security Analysis (Graham and Dodd), 130–131
Shanghai Gold Exchange, 145
Share buy backs, 131–132
Shiller, Robert, 60–61
Siegel, Jeremy, 132
Silver, 187–190
  GoldMoney and, 164–165
Silver Institute, The, 189
Singapore, 134
Situr, 25
SLV (iShares Silver Trust), 190
Snow, John, 12
Social Security, 12–14
South Africa:
  cost of gold production in, 143–144
  gold coins of, 149, 153
South Korea, 134
Spain:
  gold sales and, 5
  unbalanced consumption in, 88
Sperling, Gene, 64
St. Gaudens coins, 172, 173, 176–180
State Street Global Advisors, 161–162
Stocks:
  in China, 122
  compared to store of gold, 137–138
  gold's inverse relationship to, 110, 125

  of mining companies, 159–161, 166
  U.S. dollar and, 123
  valuation and current risk, 116–117, 130–135
Subprime mortgages, 4, 20
  derivatives and, 119
  lending standards and, 57–61
  negative amortization and, 53–56
  U.S. economy's health and, 49–52
Switzerland, 142, 177

T

Tao, Dong, 122
Telephone, buying gold over, 158
Temin, Peter, 83
Term at the Fed, A (Meyer), 81–82
Thailand, 25
Three Dollar Gold Piece, 177
Thrift, paradox of, 19
Travers, Scott, 171
Treasury bonds, yield on U.S., 26, 60, 128–129
Trichet, Jean-Claude, 118
Turk, James, 164
Twain, Mark, 160

U

United States, *see also* U.S. dollar; U.S.
     national debt
  economy of, 45–52, 75–86
  gold coins of, 149, 150, 153, 155, 156, 172,
     174, 181
  gold reserves of, 141, 142
  silver coins of, 172
U.S. dollar
  decline of, as catalyst for gold rally,
     113–116
  end of Gold Standard and current account
     deficit, 23–33
  global monetary system and, 2
  gold as protection against devaluation
     of, 110
  gold reserves and, 140
  reasons for and effects of devaluation of,
     98–106, 192–197
  value versus world currencies, 97–98
U.S. national debt, 11–14
  current account deficit and, 23–33
  as percent of GDP, 2–5
  rise of, 76
  today's level of, 41

V

Vacant homes:
  for rent, 70–71
  for sale, 69–70
Vacation homes, equity extraction and real
    estate values, 67–71
Vera, Oscar, 114
"Visibility," 131
Volker, Paul, 194
  interest rates and, 31
  recession and inflation and, 127
  on unbalanced consumption, 23

W

Wages/salaries:
  home equity extraction and, 64
  inflation and, 96
  possibility of U.S. recession and, 76
  relationship to house prices, 53–54
  slow growth of, 16, 19, 20–21, 56, 90

Walker, David, 11, 13
Washington, D.C., 58
Wittenveen, Johannes, 38
Wolf, Martin, 194
Woodin, William, 170
World Gold Council, 161–162
World War I, 27

X

XAU (Philadelphia Gold & Silver Index), 159
Xie, Andy, 123

Y

Yuan, U.S. dollar and, 102–103, 121–123,
    193–194

Z

Zelman, Ivy, 59
Zero-down mortgages, 50, 53, 59